MAINE

and Its Role in American Art

MAINE

UNDER THE AUSPICES OF COLBY COLLEGE, WATERVILLE, MAINE

Gertrud A. Mellon, Co-ordinating Editor
Elizabeth F. Wilder, Editor

and Its Role in American Art

1740-1963

A Studio Book • The Viking Press • New York

ACKNOWLEDGMENTS

One thing that distinctively marks the preparation of this book is the tremendous amount of enthusiasm on the part of the many people who have contributed their time, interest, imagination, facts, and photographs. They were all very busy people whose efforts on our behalf were not made easily. This is a compilation of the knowledge and generosity of museums and their staffs, private collectors, gallery directors, and individual scholars.

Our gratitude to all of them is great, and it is with pleasure that we especially mention the following:

Mr. John Alden; American Antiquarian Society; Mr. Philip Beam, Bowdoin College; Mr. Melvin T. Bender; Mr. Stanton L. Catlin, Yale University Art Gallery; Mr. Charles Childs, Childs Gallery; Mr. John Clancy, Frank K. M. Rehn, Inc.; Cooper Union; Corcoran Gallery of Art; Miss Bartlett Cowdrey, New Jersey Historical Society; Mr. John Curtis, Old Sturbridge Village; Mr. William F. Davidson, M. Knoedler, Inc.; Fogg Museum of Art; Frick Art Reference Library; Mrs. Joseph W. P. Frost; Mr. Robert H. Gardiner; Mrs. Robert H. Gardiner; Mr. William Gerdts, Newark Museum; Mr. Joseph Gotlieb, Milch Galleries; Miss Mary Graydon; Mr. Alan Gruskin, Midtown Gallery; Mr. Wendell S. Hadlock, Farnsworth Museum; Mrs. Edith Halpert, Downtown Gallery; Miss Charlotte Hardy; Mr. Francis W. Hatch; Mr. Bartlett H. Hayes, Jr., Addison Gallery of American Art; Mr. Norman Hirschl, Hirschl and Adler; Mr. Roland Howard; Mr. Pierrepont Johnson; Mr. Maxim Karolik; Mr. Rockwell Kent; Miss Antoinette Kraushaar, Kraushaar Gallery; Miss Florence Lamb; Mr. Robert Laurent; Mariners Museum; Mrs. Langdon P. Marvin; Mr. Thomas N. Maytham, Museum of Fine Arts, Boston; Metropolitan Museum of Art; Mr. Harry Shaw Newman, Old Print Shop; New York State Historical Association; Portland Museum of Art; Mr. and Mrs. Meyer Potamkin; Mr. Perry Rathbone, Museum of Fine Arts, Boston; Mrs. Helen Appleton Reed; Mr. Marvin Sadik, Bowdoin College; Shelburne Museum; Mr. Victor Spark; Mr. Henry Strater, Museum of Art of Ogunquit; Mr. Frederick A. Sweet, Art Institute of Chicago; Mr. Robert Vose, Vose Galleries; Mr. Maynard Walker, Maynard Walker Gallery; Mrs. David A. Wasson; Mrs. Perry Westerfield; Mr. John Wilmerding; Miss Eunice Wheeler.

The photographs of sculpture on pages 52, 61, 83, 90, 131, 132, 133, 166, 167, and 168 were taken especially for this book by Albert Fenn.

First published in 1963 by The Viking Press, Inc.
625 Madison Avenue, New York 22, N.Y.

Published simultaneously in Canada by
The Macmillan Company of Canada Limited

Library of Congress catalog card number: 63-12644
Text printed in the U.S.A. by The Murray Printing Company
Gravure printed in Switzerland under the supervision of J. H. Masui Associates
Color printed in the U.S.A. by Civic Printing Co.

Contents

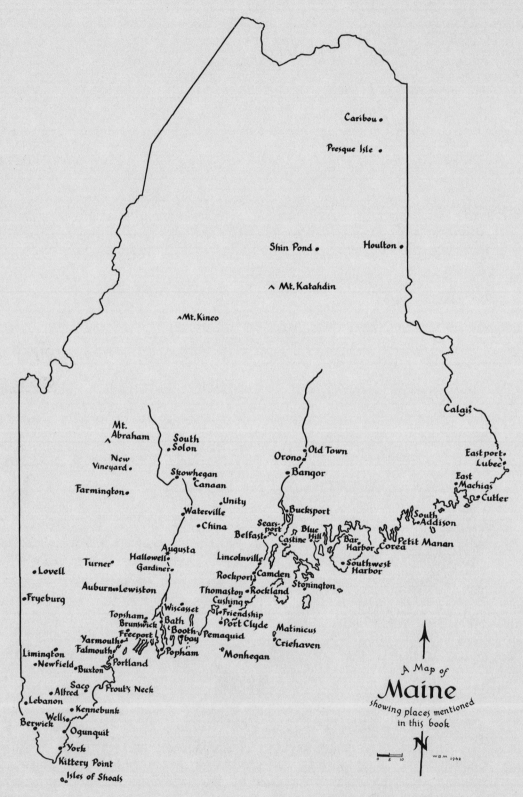

Caribou.

Presque Isle.

Shin Pond. Houlton.

∧ Mt. Katahdin

∧ Mt. Kineo

Calais.

Mt.
∧ Abraham   South
Solon.   Old Town
New   Orono.
Vineyard. Skowhegan. Bangor   East port.
Canaan.   Lubec.
Farmington.   East
Unity.   Bucksport.   Machias.
Waterville.   Cutler.
China.   Searsport   Blue   South
Belfast. Castine Hill Bar. Addison.
Augusta Lincolnville   Harbor Corea Petit Manan
Turner. Hallowell.   Southwest
Lovell. Gardiner. Rockport Camden Harbor
.Fryeburg Auburn.Lewiston Thomaston Rockland Stonington
Limington Wiscasset Cushing
Newfield. Topsham. Bath Friendship
Berwick Brunswick Booth- Port Clyde Matinicus
Wells. Freeport bay Pemaquid Criehaven
Ogunquit Yarmouth Popham
York Falmouth. Monhegan
Kittery Point Portland
.Isles of Shoals Buxton
Saco
.Alfred Prout's Neck
.Lebanon Kenniebunk

A Map of
Maine
showing places mentioned
in this book

0 5 10   WBM 1962

Map by Professor William B. Miller
Colby College

Foreword

THIS SIGNIFICANT BOOK is one of the direct results of the dedicated work of the Friends of Art at Colby. It was they who conceived the idea of assembling an exhibition to demonstrate the role of Maine in American art as a part of the observance of the Colby College Sesquicentennial in 1963. As this ambitious plan developed, under the devoted and energetic leadership of Willard W. Cummings, Edith Kemper Jette, Gertrud A. Mellon, Edward H. Turner, and Professor James M. Carpenter, there grew along with it first the notion and in time the detailed plan to publish a definitive book on Maine art, and, as a concurrent project, to establish at Colby permanently an Archive of the Art of Maine. The latter is a continuing project to be carried on through the years ahead, to insure that an accurate record of Maine art be established, and to see to it that it is kept open for scholars who wish to use its resources for research. The Friends of Art at Colby have given financial support toward the compilation of material for this Archive, and Colby College has likewise done so in granting sabbatical leave to one of the faculty, Professor William B. Miller, to enable him to spend a semester working on the project full-time.

It should be mentioned that since the beginning of the activity of the Friends of Art at Colby, the Colby College permanent art collection, which is an unusually rich one for a relatively small institution, has grown impressively. It is exhibited in a general scheme of rotation in the gallery of the Bixler Art and Music Center at Colby College, along with the many distinguished visiting exhibitions brought to the gallery by the Friends of Art, to be studied and enjoyed by the students, the community, and visitors from all over the country.

It is gratifying to the college that such exciting results have emerged from the dedicated work of an energetic group of friends. We greet the appearance of this important book with enthusiasm and with gratitude to those scholars and other laborers who made a dream of a few years ago into the reality of today.

— ROBERT E. L. STRIDER
President, Colby College

Maine
and Her Artists

A PERCEPTIVE LITTLE GIRL once said to me, "Maine is different from all the other states, isn't it? I suppose that's because God never quite finished it."

I thought then how wise she was, and I have had the same conviction whenever I have crossed the border of well-groomed New Hampshire into the tumbling pastures and shaggy woods and roadsides of Maine. It *is* unfinished, largely in the sense that beneath its strong, rough, uneven exterior it holds secrets not yet fully told. Perhaps the work of its artists has been and *is* to complete what God didn't do, or, at all events, to reveal to the rest of us His intentions and His hopes in terms both of people and of place.

Of all the states in the Union, Maine is most diverse in its topography. To coast dwellers it means twenty-five hundred miles of sea: white beaches in the west, at Wells, Old Orchard, and Kennebunk; fine harbors farther eastward in the Kennebec and Penobscot regions, Bath, Wiscasset, Belfast, Searsport; miles of open Atlantic after one leaves Mount Desert for Petit Manan, South Addison, and Passamaquoddy. The coast means also islands with delightful names, Matinicus, Monhegan, Vinalhaven, Swan's, Mouse, Pumpkin; it means as well countless indentations far inland, tidal streams making up between headlands, weaving through solitary marshlands, through rock-strewn pastures, past villages with white steeples and red barns. To the Aroostook farmer Maine means vast stretches of rich land like those of the Middle West. And to those people who live behind the coast and yet not in the far north it means countless

9

lakes— Sebago, Belgrade, Rangeley, Chesuncook, Moosehead—forests, swift rivers, and mountains—Katahdin, Saddleback, Kineo, Abraham.

Maine is diverse, too, in its history. Did Leif Ericson come to wonder at its beauty as he sailed his high-prowed ship along its coast around the year 1000? If he didn't, what a chance he missed! John Cabot must have seen it in the late fifteenth century as did, one hundred years later, those two Bartholomews, Gosnold and Gilbert. There is a spring on Mount Desert Island named for Sieur de Monts, who in 1604 clambered over its red rocks with Samuel de Champlain, the Frenchman, who gave Mount Desert its name. Those Jesuit Fathers who came in 1609 must often have been lured from their devotions or from the desire to save Abenaki souls. Still, perhaps they shared the enthusiasm of James Bryce, nearly three centuries afterward, and thought that the incredible loveliness of the island was worth many a Mass, said under the wings of the gulls and the terns!

George Popham beat the Pilgrim Fathers by thirteen years when in 1607 he established his settlement at the mouth of the Kennebec; and although his colonists there couldn't weather more than one Maine winter, which "in seven January houres had thunder, lightning, raine, frost, and snowe in abundance," they were, nevertheless, the forerunners of the state's most glorious industry when they built their own ship to take them back home to England.

Captain John Smith belongs more to Maine than to Virginia, which he left after a few years for Monhegan Island and the Pemaquid region. His was the ruling spirit among the fishing stations there from 1614 for several years. It was surely his fishermen who fed the starving Pilgrims when in 1622 they sent a man named Edward Winslow northward to get some food for the hungry families in Plymouth. When John Smith wrote in his charming *Description of New England,* published in 1616, that he would rather live in New England, which he himself named, than anywhere else in all the wide world which he knew, who can doubt that he was thinking first of the seas dashing against the Monhegan cliffs or of the waters of the Androscoggin and the Kennebec in their merry meeting? After all, he was a man of discernment as well as one of vigor.

Maine has known diversity, too, in the peoples who have striven to possess her. The French with their Indian allies fought against the English in both the seventeenth and the eighteenth centuries in the hope of keeping her for New France. (Even the Dutch from New Amsterdam are said to have looked early with greedy eyes upon Penobscot River and Bay.) The English won out in the end with no little assistance from Maine men at both Port Royal and Louisburg; yet the French have left their names here and there: Castine, Bois du Bubert, St. Croix, Petit Manan, Isle au Haut, Calais. In the last hundred years they have renewed their conquest, not, indeed, by wars, but by coming down from the Province of Quebec to make shoes and to weave textiles along Maine rivers, until today quite as much French as English is heard on Lewiston and Auburn streets and its soft, slurred accents echo constantly in Waterville, Gardiner, Brunswick, and a score of lesser towns.

10

It is in the summer months, however, that Maine experiences her most marked diversity. That season now around Maine lakes and especially on her long coastline means a lively contrast in speech, manners, attitudes; for, since about 1870 when some Harvard professors discovered the delights of Mount Desert Island, a new population has evolved which for nearly a century has provided the chief means of livelihood for our state and which, so far as one can see, will continue to do so. Now our proud towns and villages, which once bred marine architects and engineers, foreign shipmasters and famous shipbuilders, and which in their stately white houses boasted fabrics and furnishings from far-off shores, are littered with gift shops, filling stations, billboards, lobster pounds, tourist cabins, motels, diners. Their harbors, once the havens of square-riggers and the schooners of busy fishing fleets, now float pleasure craft of every sort.

This marriage between residents and nonresidents is clearly inevitable, for better, for worse, surely for richer in material gain, yet for poorer in abiding spiritual values, always beaten down or forsaken whenever money becomes one's chief concern. Perhaps it might be an easier union if the sojourners, who now flock in thousands either to tear along country and coast roads or to occupy the estates which they have built or the old houses bought from reluctant owners, knew more about the state which they find so alluring: about its long history; about its severance from Massachusetts, of which, until 1820, it was a province; about its intrepid fishing fleets to the Banks of Newfoundland; about its shipmasters, who in the late eighteenth century opened up the rich northwest fur trade and in the nineteenth sailed forth to make their home ports, Thomaston and Wiscasset, Searsport and Cutler, Bath and Rockland, better known in China, India, and the Celebes than ever New York, Philadelphia, Washington, and New Orleans were known.

We Maine people without doubt need our "summer folks," many of whom give us far better things than mere financial security. Yet in our pride we like to remember that from our own midst came a poet such as Edwin Arlington Robinson, a novelist such as Sarah Orne Jewett; that our great home-built ships once made us known and honored throughout the world; that our first colleges have strength, dignity, and beauty, on campuses both old and new. We like to recall that our farmers from Houlton and Presque Isle and Caribou, only a few years ago when trains still ran, left their potatoes to journey to Boston for a symphony concert, returning home that night in the Bangor and Aroostook sleeper, with new richness, to their fields. We cherish our predominant English descent and are jealous of our old English expressions, dating back three hundred years to Somerset, East Anglia, and Kent: we still like to say that we *sleeve* another when we take his arm; that we *tough it out alone* when we bear our troubles by ourselves; that we walk on *the edge of darkness* when we sally forth at twilight. We do not like to be called "natives," with jungle connotations, or to be looked upon as "characters," fit chiefly for recordings or television shows. We prefer the word *character* used in quite another sense; and our innate pride, often no doubt exaggerated as is always the fate of pride, makes us *think* at least that the best of us have possessed that *character* for nearly four centuries from the rugged days of our lonely fishing stations to these easier, less stirring ones of boat racing and country clubs.

Perhaps our Maine artists, both indigenous and adopted, will continue, as they have done in the past, to make our summer union with the outside world more harmonious, more mutually contributive. Perhaps, to repeat a beginning sentence, they will finish for us a Maine which God left incomplete. For art not only heightens life but clarifies and illuminates it, sheers away its dross, discovers its hidden truth. Like Plato's thinker, the artist looks upon "all time and existence" and thus can reveal to us all, as one people, those "ancient, beautiful things" which alone give meaning to everyman's threescore years and ten.

— Mary Ellen Chase

Eighteenth-Century Portraits

OF COURSE THE Pepperrell children might have been painted in Boston. From Kittery Point in one of their father's ships it would not have been a very long or difficult journey. But they were not so very young when they posed for the limner whose name remains unknown to us today. And two, at least, had presumably already set up their own establishments. Andrew, a partner with his father, was doubtless already married, for his wife is believed to be one of those represented. His sister, Mary, who had married John Frost in 1702, was living nearby in New Castle, New Hampshire. Another daughter, Margery, had married a sea captain in 1706, but four girls — Joanna, Miriam, Dorothy, and Jane — were surely still at home with their younger brother William, later the victor at Louisburg, when their father, to whom shipping was bringing comfortable affluence, apparently decided he would like to have his family painted. Under the circumstances it would have been far easier to bring the artist to Kittery Point than to see that enough Pepperrells went to him to account for the seven portraits that survive of this remarkable group (one of which is shown on page 17) — to say nothing of the three others which may have been painted. So far, no proof exists that this happened, but it's a good guess that it did and that these portraits may be the first paintings of a professional nature done on the soil of what is now Maine.

The word professional is here used only to imply a certain knowledge of the tricks of the trade, not high accomplishment, for these are routine paintings done in ac-

13

cordance with a formula which would have made them a repetitive group when hung all together in the Pepperrell mansion — as perhaps they once were. All seven sitters are shown half-length, to the right, one arm in front of the body, an appropriate object held in the weakly drawn fingers of the right hand: a book for Colonel William and a pair of compasses for Andrew, while his brother William toys with a pistol and the four young ladies hold fruit or flowers. But, as one can see from the portrait reproduced here, the artist was able to transmit the handsome Pepperrell features and undeniable charm. Jane, if it is indeed she who is represented and not Margery, Joanna, or Miriam—portraits of Mary and Dorothy are known—is a beautiful woman with reddish-brown hair, dark eyes, and a lovely bloom in her cheeks set off by her dress of rich brown brocade. The unknown artist was one of a number active in New England in the early years of the eighteenth century, but whether any of these were native born rather than temporary visitors from abroad has yet to be determined, and so far they are all anonymous. Their center of operation seems to have been Boston, where indeed, with one or two exceptions, the rest of the portraits illustrated in this section were probably painted during the course of the next hundred years.

If justification is needed for including these fine paintings in a book devoted to art in Maine, one may recall that Maine was part of Massachusetts until 1820 and can take pride in the succession of oustanding early American artists who worked in Boston from 1730 on: John Smibert, Robert Feke, John Singleton Copley, Edward G. Malbone, and Gilbert Stuart, not to mention the prolific Joseph Badger and Joseph Blackburn. During the eighteenth century much of that part of Massachusetts lying east of the Piscataqua was frontier territory with vast tracts held by landholders living in Boston, some of whom were more active than others in promoting the settlement and development of their holdings. It was frontier territory also in that here were outposts against attacks by Indians and the French. Landholders, military leaders, and members of their families posed for these Boston artists, and residents of the area took advantages of opportunities to sit for likenesses. Some of these portraits hung in Maine in the early days before being scattered to their present locations and others are now there.

"At present here is litle talked or thought of but war," wrote John Smibert from Boston in March 1745; "our forces are imbarking for Cape Bretton, four vessels of force are sailed to ly off Lewisbourg harbour to prevent any succours or provisions going in. this Expedition is a great undertaking for this Country if it succeeds wil be of great importance & be a terrible blow to France as it wil effectualy destroy their fishery & make ye navigation to Canada very dangerous, but if it dos not succeed we shal be almost undone here, for our best men, the flower of ye Country are going & ye expence wil be a prodigious sum of money." Small wonder that when the Louisburg expedition did succeed and the victors returned to Boston Smibert was glad to paint several of the leaders, including the commander-in-chief, Sir William Pepperrell. Though the artist had arrived in America in 1729 with solid training behind him, including study in Italy, this full-length portrait, showing the subject directing the

14

siege and wearing a long red coat and waistcoat decorated with gold braid, is awkward and does not do justice to one of Maine's leading citizens of the colonial period. Possibly Smibert had an assistant who was responsible for all but the head. This large canvas hung in the Pepperrell and Sparhawk mansions in Kittery Point until 1821, when it was given to George Atkinson Ward, as H. W. Foote records in his 1950 biography of Smibert, who transported it to Salem on top of a stagecoach and presented it to the Essex Institute.

More fortunate in his portrait was Commodore Edward Tyng, who had commanded the frigate *Massachusetts* at Louisburg and wrote a vivid account of the capture of the French man-of-war *Vigilant* on a foggy night when "we steer'd by the Report & flash of the Guns." He was about sixty-two at that time, and it's possible that this handsome likeness, which shows him in a long gray wig wearing a light brown coat and elaborately brocaded waistcoat, was painted earlier in England. There is no record of his having been there, but he led an active seafaring life until he was forty-eight and his first wife is said to have died in London. The portrait hung for many years in the houses of his son and his son's heirs in Portland and Bangor.

Commodore Tyng's second wife, Anne Waldo, was a sister of another of the Louisburg heroes, Brigadier General Samuel Waldo, "an accomplished gentleman, active and enterprising," who, according to a contemporary who knew him well, "had enjoyed the advantage of foreign travel . . . and was an elegant military officer, tall and portly." Others considered him ambitious and unscrupulous. However that may be, his likeness is the most colorful and effective American portrait of the first half of the eighteenth century. Like that of his friend Pepperrell the background shows the siege of Louisburg in progress but far more amply, and without the ridiculous traditional touch of a curtain draped behind a tree trunk. Brigadier Waldo, who had a house in Falmouth, now Portland, as well as in Boston, devoted great energy to the development and settlement of the 500,000 acres known as the Waldo Patent. A nineteenth-century historian stated he "hastened the development of the Penobscot Valley by at least a generation. He found the patent a wilderness; he left it containing ten flourishing plantations." During the Revolution this estate was confiscated, as his children were loyalists, but a granddaughter had married General Henry Knox, who recovered part of the estate for his wife and built the mansion Montpelier at Thomaston. There this portrait was hanging in the middle of the nineteenth century when it was bequeathed to Bowdoin College by Waldo's great-granddaughter.

In spite of the sitter's numerous trips to England there seems no doubt that this fine picture was painted about 1748 in Boston by Robert Feke, who in contrast to Smibert was presumably native born. His work of this period can best be studied in the Bowdoin College Art Museum, where four portraits of young Bowdoins by Feke, dated or datable in 1748, flank the full-length of Waldo. James Bowdoin II was probably barely twenty-one and a recent bridegroom when he posed for Feke in a brown coat, lined with white, worn over a cream-colored waistcoat richly embroidered in a deeper cream color. Heir to a large fortune, he was then on the threshold of a fine career. At its close the inventory of his estate was to list thousands of acres "in the County of Lincoln" valued at twelve thousand pounds, and the college founded in 1794 at Brunswick was to bear his family name.

In 1754, while James Bowdoin was still a young man, engaged in political and scientific pursuits in Boston, forts were going up along the Kennebec, as may be seen in the map of that year by Thomas Johnston which is reproduced on the endpapers of this book: Fort Frankfort and Fort Western built by the Plymouth Company and "Fort Hallifax Built by the Government of the Massachusetts." Governor William Shirley, to whom the map, incidentally, is dedicated, appointed Captain (later Colonel) William Lithgow to command the garrison at Fort Halifax. To get food and other supplies by sled through the snow to this outpost was a grueling task, and Captain Lithgow performed it well. He was a popular commander and is said to have "possessed a fine natural disposition, facetious and pleasant manners to rich and poor." His portrait in brown coat and green waistcoat, richly trimmed with gold lace, was discovered in storage in Boston late in the nineteenth century by a descendant, William L. Willey, and was reproduced shortly afterward in the *New York Genealogical and Biographical Record* for January 1898. The original has not been seen by the present writer, but from a photograph there seems little doubt that Colonel Lithgow journeyed to Boston and sat for Joseph Badger, the native-born artist who for a short time after the death of Smibert and the departure of Feke for parts unknown had the portrait field practically to himself in Boston. The shape of the head, the stance of the body, the gestures of the hands, and the treatment of the foliage in the background are all characteristic of Badger's work and combine into a formula he often used.

Badger's monopoly was short-lived, for by 1755 there had appeared on the scene at Boston Joseph Blackburn, with many of the tricks of the English portraitists at his finger tips. James Bowdoin commissioned him to paint his two children, and the portrait on page 20 is one of the artist's most appealing canvases. Elizabeth, dressed in white and vivacious and alert if not beautiful, sits in a natural, childish pose, with both feet, in blue shoes, thrust out before her, while James III, wearing a blue coat and red knee breeches, is a more wooden figure. As usual with Blackburn, the still life of fruit is well handled, and especially charming are the tiny birds with sharp beaks and bright eyes which look out from the bird's nest carried by the little boy in his hat.

By the early 1760s, Blackburn himself was already feeling the rivalry of the young Boston-born artist, John Singleton Copley. Thus when Nathaniel Sparhawk, who had married Sir William Pepperrell's only daughter, decided that he wished a full-length portrait to rival that of his father-in-law, it was to Copley that he turned. The imposing result must have been eminently satisfactory to the subject and it is, indeed, the most successful of Copley's full-lengths. Against the architectural background, perhaps carefully chosen from some print, Sparhawk's substantial figure, clothed in rose-colored velvet and informally posed, is well placed on the canvas. At the same time the artist has painted the face masterfully, and it leaves an indelible impression of how this self-satisfied gentleman, so "fond of coach and show," must have

16

A DAUGHTER OF COLONEL WILLIAM
PEPPERRELL (1648-1734) OF KITTERY POINT
Artist unknown, probably c. 1707-1713.

The portrait is said to be of Jane Pepperrell (1701-1765),
who married successively Benjamin Clark, William Tyler,
and the Reverend Ebenezer Turell.
*(Oil, 29 x 25 inches. Society for the Preservation of New
England Antiquities. Lady Pepperrell House, Kittery Point.
Bequest of Mrs. E. M. Lyon. Photograph courtesy of the
Connecticut Historical Society, Hartford.)*

SIR WILLIAM PEPPERRELL,
BARONET (1696-1759)
By John Smibert (1688-1751), c. 1747.

Sir William was born and lived at Kittery
Point. Shipowner, merchant, large landholder, and soldier, he was commander-
in-chief of the Louisburg expedition, and
the first American baronet.
*(Oil, 96 x 56 inches. Essex Institute, Salem,
Massachusetts.)*

LT. GEN. SIR WM. PEPPERRELL, Bart.
The Victor of Louisbourg A.D. 1745.

Opposite:
JAMES BOWDOIN II (1726-1790)
By Robert Feke (active 1741-1750),
1748.

Bowdoin, a landholder along the Kennebec, began his political career in the General Court in 1753. He was Governor of
Massachusetts 1785-1787, and President
of the American Academy of Arts and
Sciences.
(*Oil, 48¾ x 39¼ inches. The Bowdoin
College Art Museum, Brunswick. Bequest
of Sarah Bowdoin Dearborn.*)

COMMODORE EDWARD TYNG
(1683-1755)
Artist unknown, c. 1725-1750.

Tyng was a Boston merchant and sea cap-
tain whose vessels were often at Falmouth
(Portland) where he owned land and prob-
ably was born. He captured a French pri-
vateer in 1744.
(*Oil, 49¾ x 40⅜ inches. Mabel Brady
Garvan Collection, Yale University Art
Gallery, New Haven, Connecticut.*)

DR. SILVESTER GARDINER (1708-1786)
By John Singleton Copley (1737/8-1815), c. 1770.

Born in Rhode Island, Gardiner studied surgery in London
and Paris, established the first apothecary shop in Boston,
and held large tracts of land on the Kennebec.
(*Oil, 50 x 40 inches. Private collection.*)

ELIZABETH BOWDOIN (1750-1809)
AND JAMES BOWDOIN III
(1752-1811)
By Joseph Blackburn (active in New
England 1754-1763), probably c. 1761.

Elizabeth married in 1767 John Temple,
who afterward became Sir John, 8th baronet. For another portrait of James Bowdoin III, see page 24.
(*Oil, 36½ x 57½ inches. The Bowdoin
College Art Museum, Brunswick. Bequest
of Sarah Bowdoin Dearborn.*)

NATHANIEL SPARHAWK
(1715-1776)
By John Singleton Copley, 1764.

Sparhawk married Elizabeth Pepperrell in
1742. He lived at Sparhawk Hall, Kittery
Point, and was Representative to the Gen-
eral Court, Justice of the Court of Com-
mon Pleas, and Governor's Councillor.
(*Oil, 90 x 57½ inches. Estate of Frederick
H. Rindge, on loan at the Museum of Fine
Arts, Boston.*)

COLONEL WILLIAM LITHGOW (died 1798)
By Joseph Badger (1708-1765), probably c. 1760.

Lithgow, son of a member of the garrison at Fort George in Brunswick, was commander at Fort Richmond in the 1740s and at Fort Halifax later. In 1760 be became Judge of the Court of Common Pleas of Lincoln County and in 1766 built a house in Georgetown. (*Oil, 44½ x 36½ inches, sight. Photograph courtesy of the Maine Historical Society, Portland. Collection of Mrs. Charles D. Osborne.*)

ROBERT HALLOWELL GARDINER
(1782-1864)
By Edward Greene Malbone, 1805.

Born in England, Gardiner was the son of
Robert Hallowell, a loyalist, and added the
name Gardiner to his own in accordance
with his grandfather's will. He lived at and
was a generous benefactor of Gardiner.
(*Water color on ivory, 2½ x 2 inches,
sight. Private collection.*)

EMMA JANE TUDOR (MRS.
ROBERT HALLOWELL GARDINER)
(1785-1865)
By Edward Greene Malbone (1777-1807),
1805.

The daughter of Judge William Tudor of
Boston, after her marriage Mrs. Gardiner
lived first at Pittston and then at Gardiner
in two houses, both called "Oaklands,"
built by her husband.
(*Water color on ivory, 2¹³⁄₁₆ x 2⁵⁄₁₆ inches,
sight. Private collection.*)

COLONEL JAMES SWAN (1754-1830)
By Gilbert Stuart (1755-1828), c. 1798(?).

A Boston patriot in his youth, and an un-
principled financier, imprisoned for debt
in later life, Swan purchased the Burnt
Coat Islands near Mount Desert in 1786.
(*Oil, 28⅜ x 23¼ inches. Museum of Fine
Arts, Boston.*)

22

MRS. SAMUEL WALDO (SARAH ERVING) (1737-1817)
By John Singelton Copley, c. 1765.

Born in Boston, Sarah Erving married in 1762 Colonel Samuel Waldo, son of the Briga-
dier painted by Feke (see page 25). The Waldos lived in Falmouth until 1770.
(*Oil, 50 x 40 inches. Private collection. Photograph courtesy of the Museum of Fine Arts,*
Boston.)

JAMES BOWDOIN III (1752-1811)
By Gilbert Stuart, probably before 1804.

Son of Governor James Bowdoin, James III was appointed Minister to Spain in 1804 and conducted negotiations in London and Paris until 1808. He was an art collector and a benefactor of Bowdoin College.
(Oil, 29¼ x 24¾ inches. The Bowdoin College Art Museum, Brunswick. Bequest of Sarah Bowdoin Dearborn.)

MRS. JAMES BOWDOIN III (SARAH BOWDOIN) (1761-1826)
By Gilbert Stuart, probably before 1804.

The daughter of William Bowdoin, Sarah married her first cousin in 1781. Her second husband, whom she married in 1813, was General Henry Dearborn.
(Oil, 29¼ x 24¾ inches. The Bowdoin College Art Museum, Brunswick. Bequest of Sarah Bowdoin Dearborn.)

BRIGADIER GENERAL SAMUEL WALDO
(1695-1759)
by Robert Feke, probably c. 1748
Waldo, landowner in Maine, made fifteen trips abroad to
bring settlers to the Penobscot region. He died near the
site of Bangor while on an expedition to establish a fort.
*(Oil, 96 x 59¼ inches. The Bowdoin College Art Museum,
Brunswick. Bequest of Mrs. Lucy Flucker Knox Thatcher.)*

ELIZABETH ROSS (MRS. WILLIAM TYNG)
(1751-1831)
By John Singleton Copley, 1767 (?)
The daughter of Alexander Ross of Falmouth, Elizabeth
married Tyng in 1769. She went to New York and to
Canada during the Revolution, and returned in 1793 to live
in Gorham.
(Oil, approx. 50 x 40 inches. M. and M. Karolik Collection,
Museum of Fine Arts, Boston.)

looked. In fact, for the next ten years, until Copley's departure for England never to return, New Englanders would have at their service one of the finest portrait painters America has produced, as may be seen in the books by B. N. Parker and A. B. Wheeler, to whom all writers on the artist are indebted.

It may have been about 1765 that Mrs. Samuel Waldo sat to Copley. If so she would have had to journey from Falmouth for the purpose, but no doubt she went to Boston from time to time to see her father, the wealthy shipowner and merchant, John Erving, and her older sister, Mrs. James Bowdoin II. Mrs. Waldo was said by a niece to have been "as pure a human character as ever existed" but "so plain in person" her father "prophesied she would never get a husband." The artist, as is often the case, evidently understood and found interesting the personality of his sitter and painted one of his most attractive and sensitive portraits. The dress is white satin, there is a blue scarf over the shoulders, and the curtain is a dull red. The reflection of the sitter's arm in the polished table top is a favorite device of Copley's. In this case, placing the table in such a way that the sitter is somewhat protected behind it, giving her the branch of bright red cherries to occupy her hands, and directing her gaze away from the spectator may have been his way of putting a shy subject at ease.

Such observations about an artist's intentions in matters of pose and costume are risky, for, as is now well known, many early American artists, including Copley at this stage of his career, did not hesitate to use English portrait prints as models for composition and costuming. For example, when Copley painted sixteen-year-old Elizabeth Ross holding a dove he was probably inspired by a figure in a mezzotint by Edward Fisher after Reynolds, of Lady Amabel Yorke and her sister. Two years after the presumed date of this picture Elizabeth married a son of Commodore Edward Tyng. He was sheriff of Cumberland County and a loyalist. According to tradition, this and other family portraits were removed to a field for safekeeping during Mowatt's bombardment of Falmouth in 1775.

Copley was at the height of his powers when, probably about 1770, he painted the straightforward, vigorous portrait of Dr. Silvester Gardiner on page 18. The doctor wears a plain reddish-brown suit with gilt buttons; one arm rests on a table covered with a dark blue cloth, and the other is flung over the back of a fine mahogany chair. Before the Revolution he did much to develop the area which is now Gardiner, Maine. By that time, as Robert Hallowell Gardiner recorded in his *Early Recollections,* "he had cleared a farm, built a number of houses, a grist mill, fulling mill, saw mills, potash works and a wharf. . . . He had given away 50 or 60 lots . . . in the neighborhood of his mills, and had aided the persons to whom he had given them with money to erect their buildings." He had even built a ship to promote trade between the Kennebec and Boston. Though he was a loyalist and went to England during the Revolution, confiscation of this land was, fortunately for him, never carried through, and it eventually came into the possession of his grandson.

On attaining his majority in 1803 Robert Hallowell Gardiner promptly took over active management of the estate, and from then on he was there from early spring until late fall, spending only the winter months in Boston. In June 1805 he married

Emma Jane Tudor and took her by horse and chaise to the Kennebec where the young Boston woman doubtless spent many lonely hours while her husband was deep in the business of the estate. Social visits ordinarily had to be made by sailboat, but one wintry day when it was thirty degrees below zero Mr. Gardiner took his wife and baby daughter ten miles over the ice to call on relatives on Swan Island. The expedition was a great success. "I only found some inconvenience," he wrote, "from my eyelashes freezing together." The two exquisite miniatures here reproduced, showing him in a black suit and his bride-to-be in a sheer, very pale pink gown, were painted in Boston by the Rhode Island–born artist, Edward G. Malbone, probably in June 1805. At any rate, they were paid for in that month, according to Malbone's account book: "Mr. Gardner 2 pictures with settings, hair work and cyphers. 140." It was fortunate that, when Mr. Gardiner wished miniatures made, the outstanding American miniature painter of his time was at hand, paying a last professional visit to Boston before his untimely death from consumption.

Another painter of Rhode Island origin who had already achieved notable success in England, Ireland, New York, Philadelphia, and Washington arrived in Boston in 1805. This was Gilbert Stuart, who came with the intention of settling there. From the beginning "he was overwhelmed with business," wrote one of his contemporaries, and "many had to wait months for an opportunity to sit to him." A glance at the three examples of his work shown here will explain why. Within a simple format which emphasized the features of his sitters he could present them effectively as sophisticated, dignified, or witty individuals, but not at the sacrifice of resemblance. The more lively and colorful of the men's likenesses is that of James Swan, whose blue eyes and fresh complexion are set off by powdered hair, a dark greenish-blue coat and a red curtain. By the time he posed — and it may have been well before Stuart came to Boston — his efforts to settle Burnt Coat (now Swan's) Island along lines reminiscent of France's Old Régime had failed. The mill run by tidal power would soon be abandoned and his fine manor house occupied by squatters.

No greater contrast to Swan could be found than solvent, philanthropic James Bowdoin III, sedately dressed in gray. Never robust in health, he was not a well man when he was painted, as the artist has clearly shown. His portrait with that of his wife in white dress and rose-colored scarf, though bequeathed by her to Bowdoin, went to the college only in 1870, there to join the European paintings and drawings and the family portraits which, through his will and hers, had been deposited there much earlier to form the nucleus of a museum of art.

The Bowdoin portraits, though probably painted by Stuart after 1800, still strongly suggest the eighteenth century. They fittingly bring to a close this series of likenesses which well illustrate the part played by patrons associated with Maine in the development of early American portraiture.

— LOUISA DRESSER

Indigenous Art, 1700-1865

IN 1761, WHEN REVEREND PAUL COFFIN, a young Harvard graduate, left his well-established home in Newbury, Massachusetts, to spend his life as a "frontier minister" in the new settlement of Narragansett No. 1, Province of Maine (now Buxton), some of his friends considered the sacrifice too great for one of his cultural background. While the expanding years of the eighteenth century had resulted in prosperity for Newbury and other New England towns, only danger and privation had been the lot of the struggling settlers north of the Massachusetts line. Four French and Indian wars spanning almost three quarters of a century had ravaged the countryside, and these precarious times were followed almost immediately by the many hardships incident to the Revolutionary period. It was not until after the close of hostilities that lotteries, land sales, and military grants began to attract increasing numbers of young pioneering families in whose modest homes indigenous art and decoration were to assume ever-increasing importance.

Transportation difficulties between widely scattered small communities did not encourage itinerant artists to explore pre-Revolutionary Maine. Coastal travel was frequently water-borne, while inland trips were made on foot, on horseback, or by snowshoe. Horse-drawn vehicles were scarce in the back country, and Reverend Thomas Smith of Falmouth was one of the few fortunate clergymen who was able to record in his diary as early as May 27, 1745, "I set out with my wife in our chaise for Boston." Even as late as 1795 Reverend Coffin observed of Thomaston, "Here

29

saw several wagons, a rare sight." With the introduction of the first stage line from Portland to Boston in 1787, travel for all classes was greatly facilitated; a two-horse wagon, carrying passengers and mail, left Boston every Saturday morning and arrived in Portland the following Thursday. But the "golden years of stagecoach travel" were not to arrive until the second quarter of the nineteenth century.

Prosperous citizens in southern New England benefited during the eighteenth century from close social and economic ties with the mother country. It has been said that as early as 1720 there was no fashion in London that, in three or four months' time, was not to be seen on the streets of Boston. This was hardly true of coastal Maine, yet by 1740 there was in Falmouth a house — Reverend Smith's — with one room of imported wallpaper which was secured to the plaster by hand-made nails.

Although few examples have survived, pre-Revolutionary references to painted decoration are not lacking in Maine documents. In Tudor England painted wall hangings were commonly employed to enrich the interiors of small manor houses, where they served as substitutes for woven tapestries. They were constructed of heavy canvas or linen stretched on wooden frames, and were decorated by painter-stainers with scriptural, pastoral, or symbolic scenes. Wall coverings of this type were to be found in many New England homes. In 1737 Sir William Pepperrell wrote to Silas Hooper, his London agent, the following order for his Kittery home: "You have here enclosed a draught of a chamber, I desire you to geet mock tapestory or pant canvis layd in oyle to hangings for ye same, and send me." Original wall paintings in the nearby McPhaedris–Warner house, Portsmouth, illustrate this type of mid-eighteenth-century decoration.

In Massachusetts and Connecticut many scenes were painted on overmantel panels, and these comprise the earliest known group of indigenous American landscapes. This decorative fashion began to wane toward 1800, and few pre-Revolutionary examples have been found in Maine. One interesting panel, however, traditionally said to represent the environs of Louisburg, still remains in the old John Bray house on Kittery Point. It is shown on pages 32–33.

During this period young ladies of genteel families were given careful instruction in all branches of the "polite arts." These included wax, quill, and feather work; reverse painting on glass; japanning; and embroidering with crewels and gold and silver threads. While some of this needlework was taught in Boston embroidery

Opposite:
COCKEREL WEATHER VANE, Portland

This historic bird was carved in Portland in 1788, traditionally from a living model, for the old Cumberland County Court House. When the Court House was sold, the owner, Robert Hull, kept the cock, and in 1884 it was moved to the First National Bank Building at 57 Exchange Street, Portland, where it still serves its original purpose.
(*Gilded wood, about 3 x 2 feet. Collection of W. H. Clifford.*)

WALL PANEL, Kittery
Artist unknown, probably last quarter of the 18th century.

Panels of this overmantel type, from the south parlor of the
John Bray house, are seldom found in Maine. John Bray's
daughter was the mother of Sir William Pepperrell, and so
the scene depicted in the panel has traditionally been connected with the siege of Louisburg.
(*Oil on wood, 25 x 60 inches. Collection of Mrs. David A.
Wasson.*)

Opposite:
OLD CUSHMAN TAVERN MURAL,
Webster Corner
By Orison Wood (1811-1842) of Auburn,
c. 1830.

This fanciful scene is based on the type of
wall decoration painted by Rufus Porter
in a number of small Maine towns. Wood
was Porter's most outstanding follower.
Family tradition relates that he stopped at
the tavern, on the old stage route from
Portland to Bangor, and offered to paint
murals which would advertise the inn far
and near to the traveling public.
(*Tempera on plaster. Photo courtesy of
Henry Francis du Pont Winterthur Museum, Winterthur, Delaware.*)

COLONEL THOMAS CUTTS
(1736-1821) of Saco
By John Brewster, Jr. (1766-1854), late
18th century.

Beginning his career with Sir William
Pepperrell in Kittery, Thomas Cutts eventually became one of the most prominent
merchants in Maine. The goldheaded cane
is still preserved with the portrait.
(*Oil, 74½ x 30 inches. York Institute,
Saco.*)

**MRS. THOMAS CUTTS (ELIZABETH
SCAMMON)** (1745-1803)
By John Brewster, Jr., late 18th century.

These pictures are two of a group of ten
Cutts family portraits painted in Saco by
the deaf-mute artist Brewster, of Buxton.
(*Oil, 74½ x 30¼ inches. York Institute,
Saco.*)

SPRING
By Jonathan Fisher (1768-1847), Blue Hill, 1822.

A prolific reader, in the cultural pattern of the 18th century, Reverend Fisher was at
home in Greek, Hebrew, Latin, and French. He copied "brief thoughts" from diverse
sources and composed poems himself. Familiarity with French literature and art evidently
influenced his choice of this subject, with symbolic elements to illustrate the verse.
(*Oil, 26½ x 20 inches. Parson Fisher House, Blue Hill. Jonathan Fisher Memorial, Inc.*)

THE GOOD SAMARITAN
By William Deering (1741-1813), Kittery, 1790.

Identified on the back as the work of Deering, this bas-relief was carved for William Dearborn of Boston, who bequeathed it to the Dispensary as "an appropriate emblem of charity." (*Painted wooden bas-relief, 36 x 40 inches. The Boston Dispensary, Boston.*)

Left:
SAMPLE GRAVESTONE, Freeport

In this model, intended to illustrate the stonecutter's ability in lettering, ornament, and portrait sculpture, the stylized faces represent a woman with cap and a man with wig. (*Slate, 14 x 7 inches. Collection of Nina Fletcher Little.*)

Below:
RECLINING SHEPHERDESS, Gardiner
Wrought by Martha Fry Hewes, mid-18th century.

This is a fine example of the needlework pictures which were being worked by young ladies at embroidery and finishing schools in the 18th century.
(*Embroidered in silk and wool on a linen ground, 18⅜ x 25⅜ inches. Collection of Mrs. William Tudor Gardiner.*)

36

LOTTERY SIGN, Portland
Early 19th century.

This sign was owned by Major William Francis, whose office was located on Middle Street, near the head of Union; he was engaged in the lottery business about 1800. The blindfolded figure suggests Justice dispensing the riches of chance.
(Oil on wood, 40 x 30 inches. Maine Historical Society, Portland.)

HENRY BROMFIELD McCOBB, Phippsburg
By Benjamin Greenleaf (1786-1864), 1818.

This portrait is identified on the back: *Henry Bromfield McCobb, AE 7 years, 6 months. Painted by Benjamin Greenleaf at Phipsburg—May the 15th 1818.* Greenleaf painted his first recorded portrait in 1804 at eighteen years of age, and continued to paint in Maine and elsewhere for the next twenty years. His clear-cut and forceful characterizations in the difficult medium of oil on glass are unique.
(Oil on glass, 16 x 11 inches. Collection of Nina Fletcher Little.)

schools, the finished pictures, such as the one on page 36, adorned many parlors in Maine.

Three-dimensional art was not lacking in eighteenth-century Maine. Although its purpose was primarily utilitarian, it was usually executed with an innate feeling for good design. Weather vanes wrought by local artisans in wood or metal graced many barns, meeting houses, and public buildings. The handsome cockerel carved for the 1788 Cumberland County Court House belfry in Portland is one of the few early vanes still serving its original purpose.

The well-known Deering family of Kittery Point was responsible for much fine house, ship, and figurehead carving during the eighteenth century. William Deering (1741-1813) supplied ornamentation for many vessels in Portsmouth and vicinity, including the United States frigate *Congress* in 1798, concerning which the local press commented: "Mr. William Dearing has displayed . . . taste and neatness in the execution of the carved work, which is furnished in a beautiful style of neat simplicity." In 1790 Deering expertly carved and painted the unusual large plaque illustrated on page 36, representing an episode in the story of the Good Samaritan. In 1839 this was bequeathed to the Boston Dispensary, and is believed to be the only known documented example of William Deering's figure carving.

Sculpture of the stonecutter may be seen in many New England graveyards, but Maine is fortunate in having some interesting examples of portrait tombstones. Some of the faces are stylized repetitions of the familiar winged death's heads, but other craftsmen attempted to commemorate the departed by means of carefully chiseled portraits. Several of these eighteenth-century stones by an unidentified local cutter may be seen in a private burying ground off the lower main street in Freeport. Additional examples of his work, and other portraits by more expert carvers, are in the Mere Point Road cemetery in Brunswick.

Before the Revolution, Maine portraiture was largely confined to prominent families, most of whom preferred to patronize well-known artists rather than to experiment with local talent. By the 1780s, however, many "country cousins" became interested in having their likenesses taken. The pictures of Judge Jonathan and Mrs. Sayward of York, still owned by direct descendants, are excellent examples of provincial portraits of the Revolutionary period.

In 1795 two young brothers named Brewster journeyed from Hampton, Connecticut, to Buxton, Province of Maine. One was a doctor who came north to marry Reverend Coffin's daughter, Dorcas. The other was John Brewster, Jr., a portrait painter. Both were to spend the rest of their lives in Maine, and John, a deaf-mute, was soon to become a well-known traveling artist. A portrait and miniature painter of sensitivity and skill, he was working in Portland before 1800 and also in Saco, where he painted an outstanding group of Cutts family pictures (two are shown on page 34) which are now owned by the York Institute. John Brewster painted into the second quarter of the nineteenth century, and his work spans the period during which Maine art emerged from the sparse early years into the prosperity following the War of 1812.

In 1796 Jonathan Fisher, Harvard graduate of the class of 1792, took up his life's work as Congregational minister in the newly incorporated frontier village of Blue Hill. In addition to his activities as farmer, writer, and scientist he also found time to draw and paint during a long and prodigiously busy life. Pen and ink sketches, home-made wood engravings, and oil and water-color nature studies are only a few examples of the scope and variety of his work. His characterful self-portraits are of particular note, but perhaps less well known are his landscapes and a small group of unusual "fancy pieces," such as his "Spring," on page 35.

Even as Reverend Fisher was beginning his pastorate in Blue Hill, Reverend Paul Coffin was setting out from Buxton on a series of missionary journeys which would take him to scores of sparsely settled inland parishes as far north as Canaan, and as far east as Castine. In his *Journals* (published in 1855) he entered not only pungent comments on the state of religious doctrine in these isolated settlements, but also acute personal observations of the homes in which he stayed. Simple log cabins with few comforts or embellishments were still the rule in central Maine, but there were outstanding exceptions. As early as 1768 he had encountered a few two-story framed houses, one room with wainscoted wall, and windows occasionally fitted with glass. In New Vineyard in 1796 he was happily lodged in a "sweet little bedroom of logs and bark . . . well furnished and admirably pleasing." There he found, to his surprise, "Six mezzo-tinto pictures under glass; two of them are likenesses of Cotton Mather and George Whitefield." The Mather portrait was probably the Pelham engraving. George Whitefield, famous English evangelist, made seven trips to America between 1737 and 1769, when he preached and caused considerable dissension in many New England parishes. It is interesting to find reference to such pictures as these, and evidence that some of the early settlers brought what amenities they could with them.

Signboards were one of the most frequent forms of indigenous art, and in Farmington a flamboyant example caught Reverend Coffin's eye. "On one side is the brig *General Arnold,* sailing in glory on a cruise. On the other side, she is in distress, her masts cut away and the waves breaking over her. . . . Captain Coffin was on board the privateer when she was cast away at Plymouth, and was one of the fifteen survivors." An unusual early lottery sign from Portland is shown on page 37.

The work of the portraitist Benjamin Greenleaf falls within the years immediately preceding 1820, when he executed likenesses in Phippsburg, Bath, and other towns during the close of the Provincial period. Born in 1786 in Haverhill, Massachusetts, he began to paint soon after 1800, presumably to finance his education at Dartmouth. He emerged from college to become an educator of note and, in later life, the author of a popular series of arithmetic textbooks. Talented in many fields but eccentric in personality, Greenleaf used the difficult medium of reverse painting on glass to produce portraits whose characteristics of strong personality coupled with bold design were to be perpetuated in the best examples of Maine folk art during the coming years of the nineteenth century.

*   *   *

During the close of the first quarter of the nineteenth century (following eight years of depression incident upon the trade embargoes connected with the War of 1812) increased shipbuilding, foreign commerce, timber exportation, and further land development brought great prosperity to the new state of Maine. Two- and three-story dwellings began to supplant the eighteenth-century log houses. Wallpapered rooms with painted floors, woven carpets, and an occasional heating stove gave many homes a new appearance of comfort and well-being. With economic improvement came better roads, capable of travel by horse-drawn vehicles. Itinerant peddlers, artists, and craftsmen could now move about freely, and soon found ready outlets for their goods and services.

The second quarter of the nineteenth century was the richest period of Maine's indigenous art. Professional painters with little training and varying degrees of talent and skill traveled the back roads offering portraits, miniatures, townscapes, and topical scenes to an eager clientele. Although their technical ability was often slight, a flair for color, composition, and effective design sometimes resulted in pictures of great artistic merit.

Sea captains and shipowners commissioned pictures of themselves, their home ports, and their vessels, not overlooking the ever-popular side-wheel steamers. In the seacoast towns artists were kept busy depicting hazardous shipwrecks, daring rescues, and portraits of square-riggers, all of which added to the richness and variety of Maine's native art.

Traveling artists decorated signboards, and others stenciled plaster walls with floral and geometric designs. Rufus Porter (1782-1884) after six months' education at Fryeburg Academy became a traveling decorator. He and his assistants specialized in colorful panoramas of rivers, islands, ships, and hills designed to obviate the trouble and expense of procuring wallpaper.

Schoolgirls and amateurs of all ages composed scenes, still-life arrangements, and memorial pieces in a spontaneous enthusiasm for art which not only fulfilled an educational requirement but also provided enjoyment and relaxation for young and old.

Not all these artists were natives of Maine. While some were born and spent their lives there, others came in from neighboring states. All, however, painted Maine subjects, and each did his bit to provide popular art for a new and growing population.

Indigenous sculpture in the nineteenth century consisted for the most part of figureheads, tradesmen's signs, weather vanes, home-made decoys, and the usual variety of toys and ornaments whittled for the home. Little is known of many artisans who worked in small towns, and a considerable number of earlier Maine vessels are known to have carried carvings which were not locally made. Loss of figureheads by shipwreck and storm was high, and of those that survive many are unfortunately unidentified as to both vessel and maker.

John Haley Bellamy (1836-1914) of Kittery was an able carver specializing in eagles with characteristically curved beaks. His home was in the old Sir William Pepperrell house on Kittery Point, but his chief employment was for years with the Portsmouth Navy Yard. He also worked for private customers and for other shipping firms, and many of his small eagles, birds, and animals were given away as mementos to friends.

The name of William Matthew Prior (1806-1873) is one of the most familiar, and his career typifies those of many young artists of his time. Born in Bath in 1806, he advertised japanning, bronzing, and gilding together with fancy, sign, and ornamental painting in the *Maine Enquirer* during 1827. He advertised portraits and miniatures in 1828. Prices for the former ranged from $10 to $25, with frames made by himself at $3 to $10. In 1831 Prior announced: "Persons wishing for a flat picture can have a likeness without shade or shadow at one quarter price." After this date he painted in two completely different styles, examples of which are shown on pages 50 and 51, with prices cannily scaled to suit every purse.

In the country specialization was rare before 1850, and many artists combined art with more practical pursuits. Some taught school during the winter months; others, like the versatile Jonas Holman (1805-1873), combined portrait painting with theology and medicine. Born in a log cabin in Canaan, young Holman entered the Theological Department of Waterville (now Colby) College in 1824. After serving as pastor of a number of Baptist parishes in Maine, he came to Boston and graduated from Harvard Medical College in 1843. The following year he was made a Fellow of the Massachusetts Medical Society.

Before the invention of the daguerreotype in 1839, portraits were the only means of preserving likenesses for posterity. They were also symbols of status and respectability. In 1836 Arthur McArthur, a lawyer in the small town of Limington, engaged a neighbor, Royall Brewster Smith of Buxton, to paint himself, his wife, and three of their children. These pictures, one of which is reproduced on page 50, are excellent samples of the work of a relatively unknown artist of this period. Smith cannot have been a full-time painter, as the inventory of his estate mentions his farm but lists no painting materials whatever, and only two other pictures have been found that are attributable to him.

Only a few artists made permanent homes in one town. The majority traveled widely, returning periodically to the places in which they had been well received. Some stayed in the homes of their sitters; others took lodgings and advertised their presence in the local press. Many preferred the hospitality of the village tavern, where painting a signboard or stenciling the ballroom was frequently accepted in lieu of board and keep. A popular inn was kept in Alfred by one Samuel Leighton during the 1830s, and an entry in his diary under date of February 18, 1833, makes a typical reference to a traveling artist: "Mr. Lyman Richardson from Baldwin, painter, began to board at supper." Mrs. Leighton's brother-in-law passed away at this time, and on the day following his death the artist took his likeness. This was common practice in the eighteenth and nineteenth centuries. Shortly thereafter Mr. Richardson moved on to another town, and the diary mentions his painting clock faces. Barter frequently played an important part in transactions such as these. In January 1835, William Prior painted a picture of his barber in Portland and noted on the back: "Painted for three months' shaves."

VIEW OF BLUEHILL

By Jonathan Fisher, 1824.

This delightfully precise panorama shows the village of Blue Hill as it appeared in the earlier years of the 19th century. Inscribed on a rock at the lower right is the legend: *A morning View of Bluehill/Village Sept. 1824 Jon Fisher pinx.* Reverend Fisher was Congregational minister in Blue Hill for fifty years. His church, with parsonage at the left beyond, may be seen in the center of the picture.

(Oil, 24½ x 51¾ inches. Collection of Roland M. Howard.)

LITTLE GIRL WITH PUPPY
By Jonas Holman (1805-1873), 1833.
Born in Canaan and trained at Waterville (now Colby) College, Holman was a Baptist clergyman, physician, and portrait painter. A companion picture of this child's father is signed by Holman and dated 1833.
(Oil, 31 x 27 inches. Collection of Nina Fletcher Little.)

Opposite:
CAPTAIN FARNHAM, Farnham Point
In the manner of Sturtevant J. Hamblen, c. 1838.

Hamblen, brother-in-law of William Matthew Prior, was a member of a large family of painters; they lived in Portland before they all moved to Boston in 1841. Hamblen's style is hard to distinguish from Prior's. Vessels and spyglasses were often introduced, as here, in portraits of sea captains of the period.
(Oil, 27 x 22 inches. American Heritage Collection, Colby College, Waterville.)

46

STEAM PACKET *BANGOR*
By Clement Drew (c. 1806-1889), 1836.

Built in 1833 by the Boston and Bangor Steamship Company, this 160-foot sidewheeler was rigged with fore and aft sails in addition to her wood-burning engine. In season she carried about 120 through passengers a day between Boston and Bangor at a fare of $6 each. In 1842 she was sold to the Turkish government. Clement Drew, who signed the painting, was a Boston artist who painted many local vessels, lighthouses, and seascapes off the New England coast.
(*Oil, 17 x 27 inches. Mariner's Museum, Newport News, Virginia.*)

Opposite page, bottom:
WRECK OF THE *HANOVER* AT THE MOUTH
OF THE KENNEBEC
Artist unknown, c. 1849.

Laden with salt, the *Hanover* was homeward bound to Bath on November 10, 1849. Failing to clear Pond Island she was cast away and stove to pieces; all on board were lost.
(*Oil, 28 x 40 inches. Penobscot Marine Museum, Searsport.*)

Below:
SHIP *CHARLOTTE W. WHITE*
By Percy A. Sanborn (1849-1929), c. 1860.

Built at Belfast in 1858, the trading vessel *Charlotte W. White* was skippered at one time by Benjamin F. Pendleton, one of five sea-captain brothers of Searsport. Percy Sanborn, painter of this fine local portrait, spent his life in Belfast, where he was well known for his pictures of ships. He is also remembered for his paintings of Angora cats and for his musical ability.
(*Oil, 25 x 38 inches. American Heritage Collection, Colby College, Waterville.*)

VIEW OF EAST MACHIAS
By Mathuren Arthur Andrieu (d. 1896),
1855.

Machias was settled in 1763 and East Machias was a well-settled town in the mid-
19th century. The artist Andrieu was a
native of France and a portrait, landscape,
and scenery painter. Although he exhibited panoramas in Charleston, New Orleans, and St. Louis, this is the only
recorded example of his work in Maine.
(*Oil, 7½ x 63 inches. Sturdivant Library,
East Machias.*)

MISS MARY FURBER
Artist unknown, c. 1835.

Born in Portsmouth, New Hampshire, in
1795, Miss Furber later made her home
in Eliot, Maine. Despite certain amusing
deficiencies in anatomy and perspective,
this unidentified artist has contrasted his
masses of light and dark in a most effective manner.
(*Water color, 25½ x 20 inches. M. and
M. Karolik Collection, Museum of Fine
Arts, Boston.*)

THE EMERY FAMILY,
North Berwick
By Joseph H. Davis (active 1832-1837), 1834.

The profile figures of Joseph and Sarah Ann (Libbey) Emery, gay carpet, and grain-painted furniture are typical of the colorful compositions achieved by Davis, who traveled in New Hampshire and southern Maine during the 1830s.
(*Water color 14½ x 14½ inches. New York State Historical Association, Cooperstown.*)

MOURNING PICTURE
By Sarah J. Moore, 1838.

Memorial pictures commemorating departed relatives were done by many young ladies at finishing schools as a requirement for a genteel education. Painted on velvet, satin, or paper, the tomb, church, and river were stock elements which are found repeated in differing forms and combinations according to individual taste. In this painting, done at Miss Rea's School in Portland, the Portland Observatory appears to be depicted at the far right.
(*Needlework and painting on satin, 27¼ x 29½ inches. Maine Historical Society, Portland.*)

MRS. ARTHUR McARTHUR, Limington
By Royall Brewster Smith (1801-1849), 1836.

Mrs. McArthur was the daughter of Rev. William Miltimore of Falmouth. On a narrow blue band at the bottom of the canvas is inscribed: *Sarah Prince M. McArthur, born February 13th 1805 Painted June 1836 by Royall B. Smith.* This portrait, with its balanced design and strong highlights, illustrates the innate ability of some untrained artists to achieve compositions of unexpected aesthetic merit.
(*Oil, 50 x 27 inches. Collection of Nina Fletcher Little.*)

Opposite, left:
A TWIN SISTER OF THE GOODWIN FAMILY, Berwick
Artist unknown, c. 1835.

One of a pair of small profiles, in which two sisters are portrayed with subtle differences of feature which accentuate their individual personalities.
(*Water color, 4⅞ x 3⁹⁄₁₆ inches. M. and M. Karolik Collection, Museum of Fine Arts, Boston.*)

Opposite, right:
ELIZABETH WOODBURN COFFIN, Buxton
Artist unknown, c. 1830.

The granddaughter of Rev. Paul Coffin, Miss Elizabeth's delicate miniature is typical of many advertised and painted by traveling artists.
(*Water color on paper, in original gold carved frame, 2½ x 1⅞ inches. Collection of Nina Fletcher Little.*)

MRS. NANCY SNOW (WIFE OF CAPTAIN JOHN SNOW), Bath
Attributed to William Matthew Prior (1806-1873), c. 1846.

The extraordinary linear quality of pictures such as this was achieved with a minimum of time and effort. Offered to prospective customers as "flat" likenesses, they were sometimes priced as low as $2.92 including frame and glass, and required only about an hour's sitting.
(*Oil, 14¼ x 10¼. Webb Gallery, Shelburne Museum, Shelburne, Vermont.*)

MRS. HENRY BRAGDON, Portland
By William Matthew Prior, 1838.

Inscribed *Mrs. Bragdon Painted by W. M. Prior, Portland, Jan. 12, 1838 in Market Square*, this is a handsome, well-modeled portrait, effectively posed and lighted. It is typical of Prior's best early work in Maine. The picture of Mrs. Nancy Snow on the opposite page illustrates his rapid and less costly style.
(*Oil, 32 x 28 inches. Collection of Maxim Karolik.*)

EAGLES WITH SHIELDS
By John Haley Bellamy (1836-1914), Kittery Point, 1875.

Bellamy specialized in eagles of all sizes, from the huge figurehead of the U.S.S. *Lancaster* (Mariner's Museum) to small examples for a variety of decorative purposes. The wings of each figure are carved from a single piece of natural pine. The shield, eye, tongue, and beak are painted in colors. The sharply curved beak is an outstanding characteristic of this carver's work.
(*Pine, 9 x 41½ inches. Webb Gallery, Shelburne Museum, Shelburne, Vermont.*)

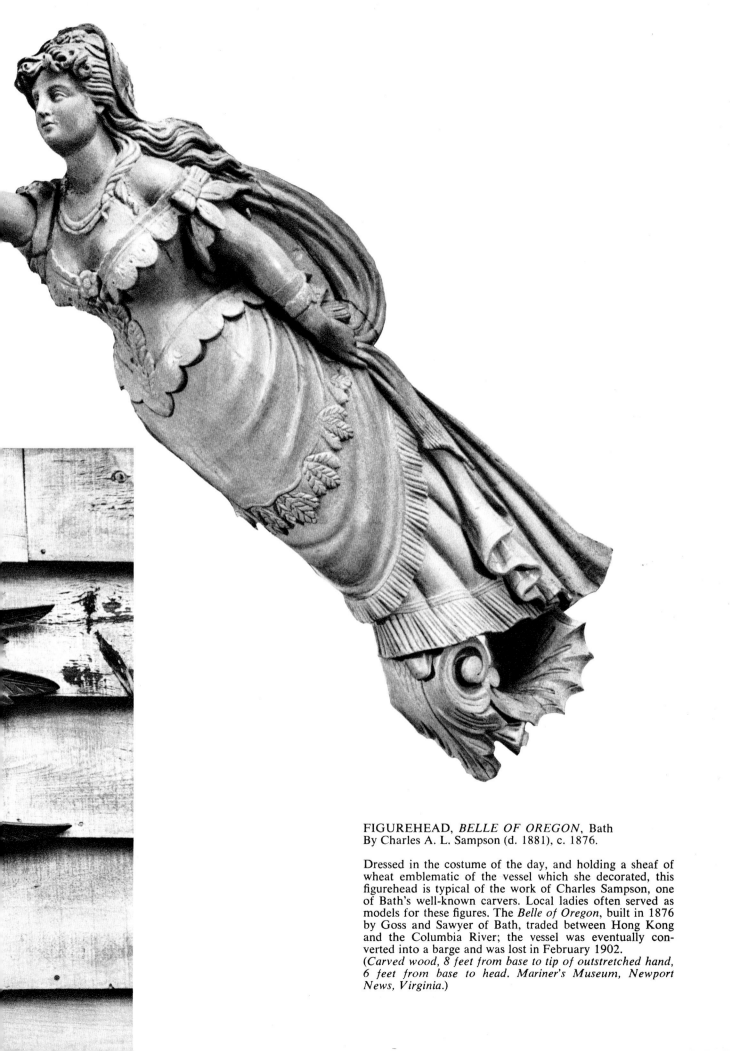

FIGUREHEAD, *BELLE OF OREGON*, Bath
By Charles A. L. Sampson (d. 1881), c. 1876.

Dressed in the costume of the day, and holding a sheaf of
wheat emblematic of the vessel which she decorated, this
figurehead is typical of the work of Charles Sampson, one
of Bath's well-known carvers. Local ladies often served as
models for these figures. The *Belle of Oregon*, built in 1876
by Goss and Sawyer of Bath, traded between Hong Kong
and the Columbia River; the vessel was eventually converted into a barge and was lost in February 1902.
(*Carved wood, 8 feet from base to tip of outstretched hand,
6 feet from base to head. Mariner's Museum, Newport
News, Virginia.*)

ENTERTAINMENT OF THE BOSTON RIFLE
RANGERS BY PORTLAND RIFLE CLUB IN
PORTLAND HARBOR, AUGUST 12, 1829
By Charles Codman (1800-1842), 1830.

The painting shows Portland's Eastern Promenade, with the
Observatory to the left and Casco Bay in the background.
(*Oil, 24½ x 32⅜ inches. Brooklyn Museum, Brooklyn.*)

BURNING OF THE OLD SOUTH CHURCH, Bath
Artist unknown, c. 1854.

One of a series of three paintings depicting the destruction
of the church by a mob of "Know Nothing" party members
who on the evening of July 6, 1854, entered and broke windows, rang the bell, and set fire to the building. Two companion pictures are owned by the Maine Historical Society.
(*Oil, 18⅜ x 24 inches. National Gallery of Art, Washington,
D.C. Gift of Edgar William and Bernice Chrysler Garbisch
from their collection of American primitive paintings.*)

Above:
OLD STATE HOUSE, Augusta
By Charles Codman, 1836.

This picture was painted by Codman fo
Governor Robert P. Dunlap of Brunswick
and illustrates the artist's "realistic" style
It was purchased by the state from Dunla
descendants in 1901 and now hangs in th
State Library. The building was altered t
its present form in 1909-1910.
(*Oil, 23½ x 34½ inches. State of Maine.*

PACKING THE CATCH, Bucksport
By William P. Stubbs (1842-1909),
c. 1858.

This gives a rare view of old-time smelt
tents awaiting another season's ice. "Billy"
Stubbs was a native of Bucksport, where
he began to paint at an early age. He later
became well-known in Boston.
(*Pastel, 22 x 27 inches. Collection of Nina
Fletcher Little.*)

55

Artists moved about by any available means — on foot or horseback, by water, or in a wagon. After 1850 Prior even used the trains to transport his canvases to a central depot where he was able to store them in a large chest while he carried what he could on foot. John Brewster, the deaf-mute itinerant from Buxton, used the coastal steamers whenever possible. In March 1823 he visited Thomaston, and one of his sitters, Hezekiah Prince, Jr., made the following note in his diary: "A fine day with the wind westerly, had to set quite steady the most of the day for the painter to sketch my countenance." When the early "steemboat Main" came up the Georges River on July 28, 1824, he wrote: "the first steem vessel ever boarn on its waters [carried] among the number Mr. Brewster, the deaf and dumb portrate painter."

The life of a traveling artist was hardly an easy or sheltered one in nineteenth-century Maine, and so one hears with surprise of a woman who at times followed that profession. Miss Susan Paine (1792-1862) of Providence spent many months in Portland and vicinity from 1828 to 1831, but she apparently traveled as well. On one occasion she so endeared herself to the John Lanes of Bonny Eagle (West Buxton), with whom she boarded while painting the family, that their next daughter was named in her honor, Susan Maria Paine Lane. A portrait of an unknown lady in the Portland Museum of Art is attributed to Susan Paine.

Distinctive portraits were also produced in water color by both professionals and amateurs. Joseph H. Davis, a left-handed painter about whom relatively little is known, traveled in eastern New Hampshire and southern Maine and painted a stylish and colorful group of full-length profiles between approximately 1832 and 1837.

Some of his earliest pictures are dated at Newfield, and he worked south through Lebanon and Berwick in the early 1830s.

Water-color miniatures on paper were advertised by many artists at half price but unfortunately were seldom signed. Those of the piquant Miss Goodwin of Berwick and charming Elizabeth Coffin of Buxton, both on page 51, are luckily identified by family tradition, but many other beguiling examples remain anonymous as to both artist and sitter.

Maine is fortunate in having preserved an unusually large number of townscapes painted by indigenous artists during the middle of the nineteenth century. Included among these are views of Waterville, Skowhegan, Bath, Castine, Cutts Island, and Bird Harbor. The large canvas by M. A. Andrieu (page 48) shows East Machias as it appeared in the prosperous 1850s, with a ship on the ways, logs floating down the river, and a spanking stage coach rattling down the main street. Some of the buildings depicted are still standing — Washington Academy on the hill with the Baptist Church facing it across the river, and the dark Congregational Church looming in the right background.

Charles Codman (1800-1842), who began his career in Portland as an ornamental painter of walls, fireboards, and other decorative work, is now best known for his romantic and picturesque landscapes. On occasion, however, he reverted to a realistic style which is as gay and charming as it is unexpected. His view of the old State House in Augusta, reproduced on page 55, shows the building as originally designed by Charles Bulfinch and completed in 1831. Two of the adjacent houses, including the Blaine mansion, still remain. Although Codman, like most of his contemporaries, derived inspiration from printed sources, his "Entertainment of the Boston Rifle Rangers" proves him a spirited recorder of this local event which took place on Portland's Eastern Promenade in August 1829.

About 1836 Esteria Butler (1814-1891), a talented amateur who probably received elementary drawing instructions in her father's popular school for young ladies, painted the interesting oil shown on page 56, of the early buildings of Waterville (Colby) College, of which the Reverend Butler was a trustee from 1826 to 1855. All these naïve landscapes, painted with the factual eye of long acquaintance, have happily caught and preserved for this generation the essence of nineteenth-century Maine.

Genre subjects of this period in American folk art are relatively rare, but one occasionally encounters a graphic representation of a local incident which caught the painter's fancy. The once familiar bustle of packing the spring catch in Bucksport, Furbish's exciting dash to Montreal by sleigh in 1845 to prove the superiority of the proposed Portland railroad route over that being promoted by Boston, the spectacular destruction of Bath's Old South Church on the evening of July 6, 1854 — all are valuable pictorial records of contemporary life and events.

Gradually, however, the machine began to displace the handwork of the artisan. Iron ships eventually rendered carved figureheads obsolete, and new photographic processes gradually superseded the uncertain brush of the itinerant. The wide distribution of cheap lithographs also played a part in directing the popular taste for art into new channels. Innkeeper Leighton noted in his diary even before 1850: "In October I paid a pedlar 62½ cents for the [lithographs of] ten Presidents." By the close of the Civil War another era had dawned in the art of Maine.

— NINA FLETCHER LITTLE

The contemporary records cited in the foregoing chapter include *Journals of the Rev. Thomas Smith and the Rev. Samuel Deane,* edited by William Willis (Portland, 1849) and *The Memoir and Journals of Rev. Paul Coffin, D.D.,* edited by Cyrus Woodman (Portland, 1855); the diary of Samuel Leighton is quoted by Margaret H. Jewell in "Country Life in Maine a Century Ago," *Old Time New England*, XXIII, No. 2 (October 1932); the diary of Hezekiah Prince, Jr., of Thomaston, is unpublished. Other sources of primary material are *The Furniture of Our Forefathers* by Esther Singleton (New York, 1901), *American Figureheads and Their Carvers* by Pauline A. Pinckney (New York, 1940), and *Annals of the Town of Warren* by Cyrus Eaton (1851).

Painting and Sculpture, 1820-1865

HENRY T. TUCKERMAN, whose *Book of the Artists* (1867) was the most inclusive and representative work on what was then contemporary American creation, expressed little surprise that artists should emerge from the Ohio Valley or from even more recently settled parts of the West. But Maine was another matter! That the sculptor Paul Akers had been born at Saccarappa and raised at Salmon Falls (only a few miles from Portland) made Tuckerman marvel at "the obscure and isolated unfolding" of a "gifted soul" in such a "scene of primitive toil."

Akers' concern with working in the round was encouraged by his father's "toil": the parent was a wood turner, and the lad executed on the family lathe "original designs," "beautiful toys." However, the sculpture of his mature years was not a further outgrowth of his environment but rather the most promising of successive efforts to escape. While still young, he had substituted Paul for his given name, Benjamin, in acceptance of the jeers of his contemporaries who, angered by his criticism of their games and their profanity, had mocked him as "St. Paul."

Sculpture was then the most exotic of American arts: its practitioners commonly resided in Italy, where marble and assistants skilled at fashioning it were easily available. Although Akers modeled many portrait heads in Washington, D.C., he carried the clays to Florence to be "finished in marble." His ambitious works — "Una and the Lion," "Diana and Endymion," "Lost Pearl-Diver" — were completely executed abroad in the cold, meticulous neoclassical idiom then internationally

OFF THE MAINE COAST
By Thomas Birch (1779-1851), 1835.

To contemporaries of Birch this scene suggested a "frontier"
rather than a place for summer vacationing.
(*Oil, 39½ x 59½ inches. Fruitlands Museum, Harvard,
Massachusetts.*)

Below:
DESERT ROCK LIGHTHOUSE, Mount Desert
By Thomas Doughty (1793-1856), 1847.

Doughty's painting, with its carefully contrived realism,
anticipates by more than a hundred years the subsequently
popular motif of the Maine lighthouse.
(*Oil, 27 x 41 inches. Collection of the Newark Museum,
Newark, New Jersey.*)

VIEW OF CAMDEN
By Alvan Fisher (1792-1863), undated.

When the expedition of George Waymouth reached the Maine coast in the spring of 1605, it was, according to historians, the region near Camden that was described by James Rosier: "The farther we went, the more pleasing it was to every man, alluring us still with the expectation of better."

(*Oil, 36 x 27¼ inches. Collection of Philip Hofer.*)

SUNSET, 1856
(*Oil, 24 x 36 inches. Munson-Williams-Proctor Institute, Utica, New York.*)

TWO LANDSCAPES BY FREDERIC E. CHURCH (1826-1900)

Opposite:
MOUNT DESERT, 1851
(*Oil, 17 x 24 inches. Collection of R. Amory Thorndike.*)

Church, a pupil of Thomas Cole, rendered natural details in his paintings with amazing precision. His *Sunset* is an orchestration in light and color; in *Mount Desert* clarity and intensity are heightened almost to the point of surrealism.

DESERTED HOUSE ON MOUNT DESERT ISLAND
By Thomas Cole (1801-1848), c. 1845.

Cole's romantic soul responded here not to scenic grandeur
but to the mutability of earthly things as manifested by
humble beginnings in the newest part of the world.
(*Oil, 17½ x 23½ inches. Fogg Art Museum, Harvard
University, Cambridge, Massachusetts.*)

VIEW OF CASTINE, MAINE
By Fitz Hugh Lane (1804-1865), 1850.

The view is from the town, which slopes down to the deep harbor. Blue Hill is at the left.
(Oil, 21 x 33 inches. Collection of Maxim Karolik.)

THE MOOSE HUNTER
By Charles Codman (1800-1842), 1831.

Although the hill in the background and the enframing foliage may not represent a specific place in Maine, the artist has depicted authentically the dress of the Indian and the manner of hunting. The moose has been chased toward the water, where it is forced to slow down and the kill is made easier.
(Oil on wood panel, 23¾ x 32¼ inches. Collection of Victor Spark.)

Overleaf:
BLUE HILL, MAINE
By Fitz Hugh Lane.

By comparison with Jonathan Fisher, whose view of Blue Hill is shown on page 43, Lane presents a greater panorama. (*Oil, 20 x 30 inches. Private collection.*)

Below:
PIC NICK
By Jerome B. Thompson (1814-1886), c. 1850.

This painting, originally attributed to Jeremiah P. Hardy, was once thought to represent a setting near Camden. The oak trees, the coast line, and the island at the right seem to correspond to the topography at Sherman's Point, where there is a long tradition of picnicking. However, now that the work has been reattributed to Thompson, its locale is no longer certain.
(*Oil, 41 x 62 inches. M. and M. Karolik Collection, Museum of Fine Arts, Boston.*)

**CATHERINE WHEELER
HARDY AND HER
DAUGHTER**
By Jeremiah Pearson Hardy
(1800-1887), c. 1842.

Hardy posed his wife and daughter against the view from their
house on the Penobscot River.
Annie Eliza—about three years
old at the time—became a painter
of still lifes.
*(Oil, 29¼ x 36 inches, M. and
M. Karolik Collection, Museum
of Fine Arts, Boston.)*

MRS. MELLON AND SON
By Joseph Greenleaf Cole
(1806-1858), 1828.
*(Oil, 35¾ x 27¾ inches. Black House,
Ellsworth.)*

A YOUNG LADY OF PORTLAND
By Charles Octavius Cole
(1814(?)-1858), 1843.
*(Oil, 29½ x 24½ inches. Colby College,
Waterville.)*

THE REVEREND SILAS ILSLEY
Artist unknown, c. 1840.

A graduate of Waterville (Colby) College in the class of
1834, Ilsley served several Baptist parishes in Maine, New
York, and Vermont.
(*Oil on wood panel, 33 x 26¼ inches. Colby College,
Waterville.*)

ABRAHAM HANSON
By Jeremiah Pearson Hardy, c. 1825.

Hanson, a colored barber, came to Bangor in 1825. According to the *Annals of Bangor*, by Judge John E. Godfrey, "He possessed much humor . . . and, as he afforded amusement to his customers, he was well patronized, and deemed worthy to have his portrait painted by Hardy."
(*Oil, 24½ x 21½ inches. Addison Gallery of American Art, Phillips Academy, Andover, Massachusetts.*)

SARAH MOLASSES
By Jeremiah Pearson Hardy, 1825.

Hardy painted several portraits of the Penobscot Indians who lived near Bangor. Sarah was one of the many children of John Neptune, Lieutenant Governor of his tribe.
(*Oil, 31 x 25 inches. Tarratine Club, Bangor.*)

rampant. Akers returned to Maine only when, too sick for further expatriation, he was slipping toward his early demise. His "Reuel Williams" seems to date from this final phase of his career.

The other Maine-born sculptor to achieve distinction between 1820 and 1865, Edward Augustus Brackett, was less addicted to Italy than Akers, but no more addicted to the region of his birth. Brackett began his professional career in the Ohio Valley, at Cincinnati, and settled eventually in Boston. It was too much to expect that sophisticated sculpture, then in the United States no more than an emerging art, should take its baby steps in the new, northeasternmost state.

Among American arts, painting had been the first to achieve true stature. The dominant mode had been portraiture, and the greatest portraitists of all had worked in Boston, the capital of Maine as long as that future state remained part of Massachusetts. Thus, as Miss Dresser has revealed in the chapter on portraits, there hung on northeastern walls major American works from the days of Smibert through the long career of Stuart.

The 1820s, the decade that opened with the granting of separate statehood for Maine, witnessed other important changes that were to affect art in the new political entity. Stuart's death in 1828 was symbolic: he had been the last leading American painter to specialize gleefully in portraiture, and he left behind him no important artist who was enjoying a productive career in Maine's neighbor, Boston. With dramatic suddenness the artistic spotlight was swinging away from Maine, to the banks of the Hudson. The Erie Canal had just begun disgorging into that river a direct flow from the Great Lakes which carried to New York City the produce of the West, creating the permanent national metropolis on lines of trade that passed New England by. And in 1825, the year that the canal opened, Thomas Cole showed in the window of a New York frame shop three views painted along the Hudson in the Catskill Mountains. These electrifying canvases presaged a green tide of landscape painting that was to sweep across the nation. New York had replaced Boston as the artistic capital of the United States. The portrait was ailing: long live the Hudson River school!

At its most typical, that school sought extreme naturalism, wished to depict as exactly as possible the specific characteristics of each local American prospect. This was radical practice in the early nineteenth century, when accepted theory both here and in Europe preached that landscape must be heightened and generalized to be worth painting.

The old taste which the Hudson River school superseded is exemplified by two pictures reproduced on pages 62 and 63. Philadelphia-trained Thomas Birch shows us a coast scene which, although identified as Maine, might have been painted anywhere in the Western world, since the rocks, the waves, and the boats are not rendered from direct observation but are rather the clichés of an international romantic marine tradition. The contribution of Boston's own Alvan Fisher is fresher, and indeed, delightful, but no more realistic. Fisher has used Camden Harbor as little more than a theme around which to improvise gracious shapes.

Thomas Doughty played a transitional role in American landscape development.

He had done much to set the Hudson River school rolling, through his influence on Cole, but once the new aesthetic was in full motion he could no longer compete. He eventually retired to that sinking art center, Boston, which remained faithful to "idealized" pictures while naturalism conquered elsewhere. From there he made trips to nearby Maine. Doughty's "Desert Rock Lighthouse," on page 62, is one of the most realistic of his paintings, yet the composition, mounting in such calculated steps to the lighthouse past rocks and figures, is more clearly contrived than the Hudson River aesthetic preferred.

Although the Hudson River school became the national landscape manner, practiced by artists from all over the nation even if resident in New York City, it specialized in depicting a restricted area. Maine was outside the usual beat. Asher B. Durand spoke for most of his colleagues when he expressed disapproval of those important exceptions who, as he put it, "make long journeys in search of the picturesque in order to gain attention and win applause, when by the common roadside . . . nature has furnished elements . . . more essentially beautiful." It was the exceptions who painted Maine.

Cole, although the founder of the school, was not completely of it, as he was never altogether convinced that nature was in its essence beneficent, a moral force reflecting the face of God. Cole was always searching for something nobler than "the common roadside." He painted philosophical and historical allegories which were entirely beyond the school's usual repertory, and in 1844 he made a trip to Maine. Fascinated by an abandoned log cabin in a new clearing, he applied to this pristine world in his "Deserted House on Mount Desert Island," page 65, that elegiac mood, that romantic melancholy at the passing of time and the mutability of man which he had applied to Old World grandeur in his five-part series, *The Course of Empire*.

Cole's one personal pupil of importance was Frederic E. Church. Like his master, Church differed from the run of the Hudson River school in not being a pantheist. However, he sought to bring meaning to nature not through Cole's allegories but with the facts of the scientist. He reproduced natural details with almost *trompe l'oeil* exactitude and combined them into compositions completely accurate for the regions painted, even if light and form were often caught at their most extreme, as in the paintings reproduced on pages 64 and 65. Being at heart an explorer, he preferred to find his subjects away from beaten paths. He hunted volcanos in South America and icebergs in far northern seas; he was the first leading landscapist to make many trips to Maine.

Church, a painter of many more strengths and skills than is commonly recognized, was the most accomplished artist to depict Maine before the arrival of Winslow Homer, but he was not as closely identified with the state as Fitz Hugh Lane, a far less accomplished technician of less power but possessed of great charm. Lane usually worked out of his birthplace, Gloucester, Massachusetts. One may postulate that he would have become a full-fledged (and leading) member of the Hudson River school had he not from childhood been a cripple, tied to crutches or wheelchair. He did not, with the other most gifted landscapists, migrate to New York City; the long tramps through the Catskills that were obligatory for the school were outside his possibilities — but on the deck of a boat he moved with delightful freedom. He haunted the coast of Maine, with such results as those shown on pages 66, 68-69, and 77.

The seeds of Lane's style were old-fashioned and lowly. Trained as a lithographer, he continued to practice that trade simultaneously with painting, and he concentrated on what had long been for printmakers a salable staple: harbor views containing boats and showing in the foreground recognizable landmarks, often towns embellished with human action. This vernacular mode Lane glorified with a clear, breathless poetry, with subtle renditions of light and air that certainly grew out of his own temperament, and probably also from the example of such Hudson River school leaders as John F. Kensett, who painted many coast scenes although rarely northeast of Rhode Island.

Next to landscape in the hearts of mid-century Americans were those depictions of ordinary life known as "genre." A leading practitioner, Eastman Johnson, was born in Maine during 1824, but, as he did not do much work there until after 1865, his career is reserved for a succeeding chapter. In the present chapter, genre is represented only by a Maine picnic, the achievement of Massachusetts–born and New York–based Jerome B. Thompson. Thompson's style both profits and suffers from extremely emphatic draftsmanship which invests individual figures with simplified effectiveness but destroys unity of composition. His "Pic Nick" breathes the rural warmth, the agreeable high spirits — notice how pretty are the girls — which made his paintings of sentimental genre subjects from popular poetry — "The Old Oaken Bucket," "Home, Sweet Home," "Woodman Spare That Tree" — major best-sellers when circulated in chromos.

On a professional level above purely artisan achievement, Maine had as yet developed no more than provincial painters. Her leading resident landscapist was Charles Codman, who had been trained as a decorator of clock faces, and now produced signs, fire buckets, and banners, as well as easel pictures in two styles. One style, which has already been discussed as artisan work by Nina Fletcher Little in the preceding pages, revealed the meticulous literalism of the topographical craftsman. The other was a mixture of the facile decoration which ornamental painters emblazoned on walls and tea trays with deeper conceptions based on the more romantic works of the Hudson River school. In "The Moose Hunter," page 66, we feel the influence of early works by Cole.

Although Codman largely avoided it, the likeness trade was in pre–Civil War times the financial backbone of Maine's more ambitious resident artists. They had, it is true, to vie with outsiders, such as Boston's Thomas Badger, who made painting trips to Maine. However, the competition, in the portrait doldrums which followed the death of Stuart, was not too hard to meet.

Portland's own portraitists were the brothers Charles Octavius Cole and Joseph Greenleaf Cole, the sons of a Massachusetts painter-craftsman. Charles, as his portrait "A Young Lady of Portland" shows, had the warmer response to personality, even if his forms tended to be buttery. Joseph's style is colder, but more effective pictorially. In his "Mrs. Mellon and Son" he treated his subject as if it were a still life, arranging faces, bodies, and clothes in a spare, handsome, abstract design.

A poignant reminder that talent can, like a wild rose in a hedgerow, grow and wither unperceived is given in the portrait of the Reverend Silas Ilsley which hangs at Colby College, a work of semi-naïve freshness and considerable beauty, which scholars have not yet connected with any other picture, or any identified hand.

Maine's mid-century little master was Jeremiah Pearson Hardy, for some sixty years painter in ordinary to the region around Bangor, where he had been born. He painted fecund bulls and pet dogs, town nabobs and town characters, and experimental pictures of his family, whom he loved to pose by lamplight or firelight, and also in silhouette, as shown in the painting reproduced on page 70. Hardy had worked as an engraver in Boston; he had studied in New York with the president of the National Academy and future inventor of the telegraph, Samuel F. B. Morse; but once he returned to his native ground he cultivated his "modesty" and seems never again to have carried his paints farther afield than other Maine communities. Ingenious, gay, gentle, possessed of an agreeable color sense, finding true poetry in the matter-of-fact, Hardy was one of the most engaging of the provincial American artists who in the mid-century practiced away from the centers a style balancing delightfully between the sophisticated and the naïve.

From its attainment of statehood until after the Civil War, Maine was at its most isolated from the principal streams of American art. But all was soon to change. The extension of vacationland northward brought an influx of creators from New York City and other centers: Eastman Johnson returned for the summers to the state where he had been born; Winslow Homer's family helped establish a vacation settlement at Prout's Neck. Thus was the stage set for exciting developments to follow.

— James Thomas Flexner

76

ENTRANCE, SOUTHWEST HARBOR
By Fitz Hugh Lane, 1852.
Southwest Harbor was first designated as such by Francis
Bernard, Royal Governor of the Province of Massachusetts
Bay. He became the proprietor of Mount Desert Island,
and on his first visit in 1762 he "beat in" and anchored at
approximately the spot shown in this painting.
(Oil, 24 x 36 inches. Private collection.)

VIEW OF SIMONTON'S BEACH, CASCO BAY
By John Bradley Hudson, Jr. (1832-1903), 1878.
Painted from a sketch made during the previous year, this
view of part of Portland harbor looking eastward toward
Peaks Island marks the height of Hudson's art.
*(Oil, approx. 26 x 36 inches. Maine Historical Society,
Portland.)*

The Indigenous Artists, 1865-1914

THE ORDEAL OF THE CIVIL WAR wrought profound changes in the American way of life as the nation moved away from a predominantly rural condition toward the fulfillment of the Industrial Revolution in the big cities. Caught up in this flow of events, the indigenous artist became separated from the main stream of American art, and the final decades of the nineteenth century witnessed the end of a truly native art expression in Maine. Since Colonial times the local artist had occupied a useful place in his small community, performing a variety of tasks whose common denominator was his skill at handling a brush or a carving tool. A portrait in oil paint or an effigy in wood was given the same application of workmanship that he would confer upon the decoration of a piece of furniture or the design of a weather vane. As the machine began its gradual triumph over the manual arts in industry during the period following the Civil War, there appeared a new kind of national idol — mass production. Work became specialized, and the term "jack of all trades" acquired unpleasant connotations. As Henry Steele Commager has remarked, "The triumph of standardization over individualism was a memorial to the passing of the old America." The effect upon indigenous art as a tradition was destructive in that it forced the local artist to give way before his specialist counterpart, the academy-trained painter. By the turn of the century, the time was past when the artisan who could paint pleasant decorations on furniture or clock faces was the same man who could turn with equal ease and facility to the rendering of a creditable landscape in oil on canvas. And the wood carver capable of heroic ship figureheads had disappeared with the great wooden sailing vessels as the age of steel and steam was ushered in.

One of the most impressive examples of the wood carver's art to be found in Maine today, the so-called "Portland Phoenix," shown on page 83, has a history rooted deeply in the life of that city. The disastrous fire which occasioned the carving was touched off on the afternoon of July 4, 1866, just as the city was about to engage in the festivities of the national holiday, made doubly significant by the victorious conclusion of the Civil War. Local tradition has it that some boys were playing with firecrackers near a storehouse loaded with explosives when a carelessly thrown fuse ignited material in the building. Ironically, it was a Portland painter, Joseph T. Harris, who, thirty years before, had warned of the dangers of fireworks in a series of drawings depicting the hazards of Fourth of July celebrations, published by the Boston lithographer Pendleton. The great fire of 1866 leveled half the city and left thousands homeless; but the determination to survive was strong in Portland, and in less than two months one prominent banking house had chosen an appropriate symbol that spoke for that determination. The name of the carver of the "Portland Phoenix" is not known, but it is reasonable to assume that the order for it went to a local man. One of the foremost craftsmen in Portland at the time was Edward Souther Griffin, in whose shiploft at 45 Fore Street were produced many of the large figureheads for five-masted schooners built in Maine. Griffin's father had achieved some fame as a maker of musical instruments, and a feeling for the handling of wood may well have been a family trait. The "Phoenix" reveals a strong sense of design, and, although the carver gives us a heraldic eagle mounting the flames rather than the fantastic bird of mythology, it is altogether characteristic of the American point of view. The carver has improvised upon a theme originating outside his own culture, utilizing the familiar form of the American eagle through which the symbol becomes appropriate for his own time and place.

Maine has always been married to the sea, and the lives of the inhabitants of the coastal towns of the nineteenth century were closely bound up with the building of great sailing vessels. During the decade of 1880 these towns sent out more than four hundred ships, and the times were prosperous. The portrait of Captain Phineus Pendleton II reveals a seagoing man living in the full enjoyment of good fortune. The anonymous portraitist has given us the image of triumphant enterprise. Although the style of the painting may be essentially linear, there is no mistaking the solid bulk of the figure, or the character of the sitter. The portrait of Pendleton is like many of the face paintings made in this era by a host of anonymous artists of modest abilities who reflect, to one degree or another, the appearance of professional portraiture. Nevertheless, there is still more affinity with the limner's art here than there is an affectation of academic polish. During the final decades of the nineteenth century, the art of the miniaturist capitulated before the act of photography, and further lessened the face painter's scope of activities.

If many of the regional painters no longer worked with that spontaneity which overcame technical shortcomings, there were many who applied themselves assidu-

80

ously to the speciality of their limited areas of interest. Their productions reveal a cautious development of their abilities, if not an almost scientific interest in the subject matter which they sought to depict. Franklin Stanwood, whose brief life was over before his talent had a chance to flourish, painted scenes of the ocean under varying effects of sun and moonlight. One specialist, Walter M. Brackett (1823-1919), concentrated so thoroughly upon his singular interest, the painting of fresh-water game fish, that no other subject matter has ever been attributed to him. Born in Unity, Maine, he apparently developed his talent in Boston, where he was a frequent exhibitor at the Boston Athenaeum. The memory of wilder places such as the Machias River may lurk behind the creation of "Salmon," shown in the Athenaeum annual of 1867 in the quite different company of G. P. A. Healy portraits and the romantic Italianate landscapes of George Loring Brown. In much the same vein, Alice McLaughlin (1869-1906) must have been a devoted student of the wild mushrooms which she collected in the vicinity of her home in Castine, Maine. At least fifty of these precise water-color studies exist today, evidence that her culinary art, which was renowned, did not precede a feast for the inquiring eye. In other moments, Miss McLaughlin was capable of handling landscape subjects in a creditable fashion. Her water colors are usually small, but her feeling for these scenes of coast and woodland is broadly rendered with a fine sense for the effects of light and air.

Only a few miles north of Castine, another lady painter had established for herself a considerable reputation. Anna Eliza Hardy, born in Bangor in 1839, was the daughter of Jeremiah Pearson Hardy, an artist of merit who made his livelihood from the painting of portraits. At his best, Jeremiah created pictures of great charm and felicity. Under his benign influence Anna Hardy embarked upon a painting career at the age of sixteen, and her life-long theme was the intimate world of still life. With loving precision she often delineated the peeled orange, the translucent grape, and the folded linen napkin in a manner that seems to blend the decorative qualities of a Raphaelle Peale with some of the illusionism of a Peto. Her sense of color, which was always refined, is perhaps nowhere better exemplified in her work than in "Basket of Flowers," reproduced on page 86. In the course of her long career as a painter, her power of capturing the freshness of quality which distinguishes her early paintings gradually diminished. Anna Hardy, whose life spans almost one hundred years, was born when Thomas Cole was painting the romantic landscapes which gave rise to the era of the Hudson River school. She died shortly before Picasso was to create his "Guernica." In all that time, her world remained essentially the same — a table-top world of order and beauty.

If one were to search for an individual who would most perfectly embody the qualities of the typical journeyman-artist of the nineteenth century, that person would be John Bradley Hudson, Jr. Born in Portland in 1832, he grew up as an apprentice to his father, a decorator of furniture. From the painting of chairs he turned to an interest in the fine arts, and at sixteen began a serious study of perspective and "portrait or ordinary painting" with a Mr. Harris of Bath. Upon his twenty-first birthday, when he became free to make his choice of occupation, he set out to learn more about the

81

business of painting portraits and took instruction from the popular Charles Octavius Cole of Portland. Soon thereafter, Hudson made his first journey to Boston, where he haunted the Athenaeum. In a remarkable illustrated journal now owned by the Bangor Public Library, he reports on this first experience: "Cole's Course of Empire was a splendid production and I was affected deeply by them. Allston's unfinished pictures interested me exceedingly by the beauty of their compositions and grace of outline, while the portraits of Stuart impressed me as being splendid specimens of color and expression." Perhaps inspired by this lesson he returned home and made his "first direct study from Nature." Intuition had given way before the desire to learn to see objectively; however, Hudson never did escape being a local painter, for his modest endowments did not permit him beyond this point. Throughout his career he would be known as an "ornamental and banner painter," and eventually he abandoned his art altogether.

One of Maine's most celebrated local painters of the latter part of the nineteenth century is almost forgotten today. Harrison B. Brown was a household name in Portland, and his paintings were admired and collected by most of the prominent families. Like Hudson, Brown began his career as a commercial painter. His growth as an artist is marked by a succession of advancements beginning with the opening of his first establishment on Exchange Street in Portland. By 1858 he had discarded the sign- and banner-painting business in order to embark upon a fully dedicated career as an artist. That he did not want for recognition is evidenced by the fact that between 1858 and 1860 five of his six landscapes shown at the National Academy were borrowed from their owners for the exhibitions. He received favorable criticism in the local press by such fellow artists as the sculptor Benjamin Paul Akers, and was the subject of some discussion in *Artists of the 19th Century,* published in 1899. His career in Portland was capped by his election to the presidency of the Society of Art in 1892. Looking back over the numerous scenes Brown produced during his lifetime, it becomes clear that he was at his best during the early years. His sensitive handling of thin color could produce effects of light and atmosphere that are reminiscent of John Frederick Kensett, and it was to his detriment that he became swayed by the temptation to employ thick impasto. Perhaps no other native painter of this period found so much to celebrate in the look of Maine's coast and valleys. Never a brilliant painter, he nevertheless painted pictures convincing in their deeply rooted honesty toward the nature he admired. As the clouds of war gathered in 1914, Brown was living in England in self-imposed exile, and if he painted any longer, no examples of his work from this period have come to light. Another expatriate from Maine, Hiram Stevens Maxim, also lived in London at this time, and the machine-gun that he invented helped to end the kind of world that was the only possible one for men like Harrison Brown.

The life of Franklin Simmons of Webster, Maine, completes the story of Maine's indigenous art. From humble beginnings he elevated himself to prominence, and to his contemporaries he possessed a large talent. His constant early companion and mentor was John Bradley Hudson, who notes in his *Journal* that "Frank Simmons had

THE PORTLAND PHOENIX
Artist unknown, 1866.

The rebuilding of Portland after the great fire was commemorated on August 29, 1866, when the directors of the Bank ". . . authorized Charles Rand to contract for the carving of the phoenix." Rand is presumed not to be the carver.
(*Gilt on wood, height 5 feet 1 inch. The Canal National Bank, Portland.*)

VIEW OF FREEPORT, MAINE
By G. J. Griffin (active c. 1885), 1886.

The untrained, "primitive" artist speaks directly of life in a Maine town, laying equal importance upon its economic and moral strengths, symbolized by industry and the Church.
(Oil, 21 x 39 inches. Collection of Nina Fletcher Little.)

A FIRE-ENGINE PANEL
by John Bradley Hudson, Jr., c. 1890.

One of two identical panels removed from the coachwork of a Portland fire engine, the scene represents the old Court House. After the Civil War this building was razed to make way for a monument designed by the sculptor Franklin Simmons.
(Oil on wood, 10 x 12½ inches. Portland Museum of Art, Portland.)

Opposite:
MOONLIGHT MARINE
By Franklin Stanwood (1856-1888), c. 1880.

In his short life Stanwood devoted himself to painting the sea, in various moods and in both sun and moonlight.
(Oil, 24 x 36 inches. Portland Museum of Art, Portland.)

84

VIEW OF SKOWHEGAN
By J. H. Keith (active c. 1870), 1870.

Even the beginnings of industry in Skowhegan, on the Kennebec River, lend themselves here to the romantic Italianate treatment characteristic in paintings of the period.
(*Oil, 28 x 18 inches. Collection of Willard W. Cummings.*)

BASKET OF FLOWERS
By Anna Eliza Hardy (1839-1934), c. 1870.

The daughter of Jeremiah P. Hardy, portrayed by him as a little girl on page 70, painted many still lifes of exquisite delicacy and precision.
(*Oil on panel, 11¾ x 9½ inches. Collection of William H. Gerdts, Jr.*)

Top: APPROACHING STORM: MAINE COAST, c. 1870
(Oil, 10 x 20 inches. Portland Museum of Art, Portland.)

Bottom: "OAKLAND," PORTLAND, MAINE, c. 1860
(Oil, 24 x 40 inches. Collection of John Alden.)
The seascape above (also known as *White Head*) is typical of Brown's celebration of
the look of Maine's coast. His "portrait" of the Hersey mansion, "Oakland," on Dan-
forth Street in Portland, was a tribute to his first patron, Theophilus Cushing Hersey.

TWILIGHT AT STROUDWATER, MAINE
By Charles Frederick Kimball (1835-1907), c. 1900.

Kimball was among the many gentleman painters who formed the Society of Art in Portland, and who painted pleasant views of the surrounding country. He grew to professional status after 1880, and became known especially for his etchings.
(*Oil, 15 x 21 inches. Portland Museum of Art, Portland.*)

88

MAINE BARN INTERIOR
By Harrison Bird Brown, c. 1880.

This farm scene shows the characteristic honesty with which
Brown depicted the Maine subjects among which he spent
the greater part of his life.
(*Oil, 15 x 30 inches. Portland Museum of Art, Portland.*)

HAYING AT LAPHAM'S FARM, AUBURN, MAINE
By John Bradley Hudson, Jr., 1859.

Hudson made this painting after a prolonged stay with the
Lapham family, south of Auburn, repaying their hospitality by instructing the ladies in drawing. Much of his subject
matter is drawn from walking trips throughout Androscoggin County.
(*Oil, 22 x 30 inches. M. and M. Karolik Collection, Museum
of Fine Arts, Boston.*)

CAPTAIN PHINEUS PENDLETON II
(1806-1896)
Artist unknown, c. 1865.

This portrait of a prosperous sea captain, done in the linear style of many paintings of the post-Civil War period, may be compared with an earlier portrait, that of Captain Farnham on page 45.
(*Oil, 30 x 25 inches. Penobscot Marine Museum, Searsport.*)

HENRY WADSWORTH
LONGFELLOW
By Franklin Simmons (1839-1913), 1888.

Commissioned by the city of Portland to honor the memory of its most celebrated son, this statue was cast in Italy. It is one of two public monuments by Simmons in Portland; the other in Monument Square honors Civil War dead.
(*Bronze, heroic size. City of Portland.*)

been studying and drawing and painting with me all the time he could spare from his office as clerk in the Hill Mill [Lewiston, Maine] without appearing to show any special taste for either. I finally advised him to try modeling. He went to Boston and visited [John Adams] Jackson the sculptor. On his return he made his first attempt . . . with such results as decided him to follow it as a profession." Simmons' rise to fame was rapid, and after the Civil War he had left Maine to work in Washington, where he made a series of portrait medallions of Lincoln's Cabinet and forty leading military officers. Like Harrison Brown, Simmons chose finally to reside in Europe; however, he was to work rather than to retire from activity. Rome was popular with American sculptors, and from Simmons' studio in this city flowed a succession of statues destined for the United States. Rhode Island commissioned him to execute a memorial to Roger Williams, and the Grand Army of the Republic commissioned a statue of General Grant, which he carved twice, and finally delivered in 1900. There is something sad about the first figure, for Simmons seems to have caught a mood of mourning. This statue, rejected by the Grand Army, is now in the Portland Museum, and the second is in the Rotunda of the Capitol. All of Simmons' work bears the stamp of skillful authority in the handling of marble and bronze, but none of it departs from the acceptable style of his day.

— DONELSON F. HOOPES

The Sea and the Land,
1865-1914

THE LAST THIRD OF THE NINETEENTH CENTURY was a period of enormous expansion in all fields of American life. Accumulating wealth brought increasing leisure for the upper levels of society, and made the pursuit of pleasure a major occupation. Outdoor sports and recreations, and the whole vacation side of life, assumed a new importance. The period saw the rise of the American summer resort, on a scale undreamed of in the simpler pre–Civil War years. As transportation became easier, the resort area spread eastward from Newport and the North Shore, and Maine became the favored vacation land for Massachusetts and states farther south. Soon the summer visitor became the state's chief source of revenue.

In such migrations the artist is often the pioneer. For the painter, Maine had unique resources. Its unrivaled coast, varied by hundreds of bays and islands and peninsulas, its deep fiords, its high rocky shores crowned by spruce and pine, presented a coastal landscape strong in character and rich in forms, far more dramatic than the milder coast of southern New England. And there was the sea itself, the North Atlantic with all its changing moods, its majestic storms, and its age-old, unending battle with the land.

Older marine painters who visited the Maine coast continued the romantic naturalism of earlier days. These traditionalists, of whom Alfred T. Bricher of Newburyport and New York was a typical example, had the virtues of honesty, a devotion to their chosen subjects, and sound if limited technical competence, but their

92

style inclined to be literal and prosy, with none of the romantic fire of Cole and Church or Lane's penetrating sense of mood.

A new and different voice was that of Winslow Homer. Born in Boston, his ancestry was one-quarter Maine, through his maternal grandmother Sally Buck of Bucksport. His mother, Henrietta Maria Benson, born in that seaport, was herself an amateur painter of more than ordinary talent; her water colors of flowers, captivating in their blend of naïveté and innate artistry, stand on their own merits. Her son's professional career up to his middle forties was spent mostly in New York; but he was a born wanderer, and he painted in Maine (at York) as early as 1875. In the 1880s the Homer family settled for the summers at Prout's Neck, which was then inhabited almost entirely by fishermen and farmers. In 1884 Winslow Homer built a studio on the rocky shore overlooking the sea — his permanent home thenceforth. On this rugged point of land he lived absolutely alone, often the year round. That this solitude answered a deep need of his nature his personal letters leave no doubt. "The life that I have chosen," he once wrote, "gives me my full hours of enjoyment for the balance of my life. The Sun will not rise, or set, without my notice, and thanks." Here his art reached maturity, and he painted the works on which his fame rests.

Earlier marine painters had pictured the sea romantically — a peaceful mirror, or, if stormy, with gracefully curving waves. But Homer takes us right into the battlefront between sea and shore, into the turmoil of giant waves thundering on rocky cliffs — with a directness of physical sensation, a force and vitality that were new notes in American painting. He makes us feel the weight and movement of the wave, the solidity of the rock, the impact of their collision. His seascapes are supreme expressions of the power and the dangerous beauty of the sea. And beyond that, they are design, largely and vitally conceived, in which every line and mass and color plays its part in a rhythmic, harmonic whole.

But Homer's range was not limited to marines. The weather-beaten lives of Maine fishermen and hunters, his year-round neighbors; the rocky landscape of Prout's Neck, seen in many seasons and hours and lights; the animals and birds he saw during the long hard winters, as in "The Fox Hunt" (page 102), that unforgettable image of northern solitude — all these things found their place in his art. His work was filled with a sense of the life of nature, and man's relation to it. In his years in Maine he became the greatest pictorial poet of outdoor America.

Homer's identification with the people of Maine was unusual among the professional artists who worked there, most of whom were attracted by the sea and the coast. The outstanding exception was Eastman Johnson, born in Lovell and brought up in nearby Fryeburg and in Augusta (his father was Maine's Secretary of State for thirty years). After thorough training in Germany and Holland, Johnson applied his seasoned technical knowledge to native subject matter, becoming one of the ablest continuers of the old American genre tradition. He revisited Fryeburg about 1865, and for several years thereafter returned there in the early spring, when the sap began to flow in the sugar maples and the sugar-making camps became communal, festive centers after the long winter. In the dark woods with patches of snow still on the ground, fires glowed under the big iron caldrons in which the sap was boiled down, while the whole community gathered, old men whittling and swapping yarns, young people courting, youths stealing a sly drink, men and women cavorting to the tune of a fiddle — scenes not usually associated with staid New England.

Johnson had a studio built on wheels, with a stove; and in this shelter he painted scores of studies, mostly of individual groups and incidents. There were also a few essays toward a large composition combining these studies, which he never completed. These first-hand records of scenes which must have been familiar to him from childhood carried a conviction of absolute authenticity. Their relish for native idiosyncrasies, their racy humor, their sympathy with the atmosphere of merrymaking made them almost unique in American genre art. They were refreshingly free from Puritanical moralism and from the sentimentality that marked most nineteenth-century representation of country life. In style they showed keen, unhackneyed observation, and a sure grasp of character and action. They were among Johnson's freest works in handling and freshest in color, partly because they were not carried too far but were left as direct spontaneous studies, avoiding the deadened quality of some of his more highly finished canvases. They show him breaking away from the tightness of the older genre school and of his own earlier work, toward a more painterly style.

In the 1870s Johnson often visited Kennebunkport, where his sister and her three children were spending summers. These visits resulted in several scenes, like that on page 98, of the young people playing in the old barn and its hayloft — that enchanted region for children fortunate enough to be born in the horse age. To the fresh observation of his sugar-making studies, these works added a greater intensity of mood, a tender, poignant sense of the poetry of childhood. And they showed a new feeling for the magic of light, in these little figures seen in light against the dark windowless cavern of the hayloft. The freedom of his Fryeburg work and this growing awareness of light made Johnson's development parallel to Homer's, within a more limited range.

With Johnson and Homer the old genre tradition reached maturity — and also the beginning of its end. Their absorption in the native scene was giving way to more cosmopolitan tendencies. In the picturing of Maine life they had no immediate successors of any importance. There was no pictorial equivalent of Sarah Orne Jewett's stories, with their rare combination of exact native flavor and broad human meaning. It remained for a later generation of painters to rediscover the strengths and limitations of regionalism.

An amusing skirmish in the conflict between the native and the cosmopolitan is recorded in Elihu Vedder's autobiography, *The Digressions of V*. One of the four painters from outside Maine who were chosen to execute the murals for the Walker Art Museum at Bowdoin College (the others being Kenyon Cox, John La Farge, and Abbott Thayer), Vedder was a classicist, devoted to antiquity and to Italy, but also a witty, jovial, and original mind. He and his painter friend Albion H. Bicknell (born

94

CUSHING'S ISLAND, PORTLAND HARBOR
By Alfred Thompson Bricher (1837-1908).

Bricher was typical of the marine artists who continued the tradition of romantic naturalism in their paintings of the Maine coast in the latter part of the nineteenth century.
(*Oil, 25 x 50 inches. Vose Galleries of Boston.*)

ON A LEE SHORE, 1900
(*Oil, 39 x 39 inches. Rhode Island School of Design, Providence, Rhode Island.*)

A BOLD NEW VISION: THREE OILS OF PROUT'S NECK BY WINSLOW HOMER (1836-1910)

THE ARTIST'S STUDIO IN AN
AFTERNOON FOG, 1894
(Oil, 24 x 30 inches. Rochester Memorial
Art Gallery, University of Rochester,
Rochester, New York.)

KISSING THE MOON, 1904
(Oil, 30 x 40 inches. Addison Gallery of American Art,
Phillips Academy, Andover, Massachusetts.)

TWO SCENES FROM MAINE FARM LIFE
BY EASTMAN JOHNSON (1824-1906)

Right: SUGARING OFF (No. 2), c. 1870
*(Oil, 33½ x 54 inches. Butler Institute of
American Art, Youngstown, Ohio.)*

Below: IN THE HAYLOFT, c. 1875
*(Oil, 26½ x 33 inches. Fine Arts Gallery
of San Diego, California. Gift of Mrs.
S. H. Darlington.)*

OLD PAIL AND FIREWOOD
By Elihu Vedder (1836-1923), 1865.

In search of subjects to rival those he had found in Europe, Vedder went to Turner, Maine, where he found, he said, "an old pail and some firewood, and made a careful study which I cherish."
(*Oil, 8 x 10 inches. Newark Museum, Newark, New Jersey.*)

Left: COAST OF MAINE
By Emil Carlsen (1853-1932).

(Oil, 40 x 50 inches. City Art Museum, St. Louis.)

Below: BENEDICTION
By Willard L. Metcalf (1858-1925).

(Oil, 36¼ x 39¼ inches. Collection of Lady V. Gabriel.)

THE IMPRESSIONISTS' MAINE

ISLES OF SHOALS
By Childe Hassam (1859-1935), 1901.

Hassam, a pioneer of American impressionism, spent many summers on Appledore, in
the Isles of Shoals, painting the rocks and the shimmering sea.
(Oil, 25 x 30 inches. The Metropolitan Museum of Art. Gift of George A. Hearn, 1909.)

THE FOX HUNT
By Winslow Homer, 1893.

Winter on Prout's Neck: starving crows are attacking a fox.
*(Oil, 38 x 68 inches. Pennsylvania Academy of the Fine
Arts, Philadelphia.)*

102

WEST POINT, PROUT'S NECK
By Winslow Homer, 1900.
"Painted *fifteen minutes* after sunset—not one minute be-
fore," Homer wrote.
*(Oil, 30¼ x 48¼ inches. Sterling and Francine Clark Art
Institute, Williamstown, Massachusetts.)*

RIGHT AND LEFT
By Winslow Homer, 1909.
Ducks are brought down by two shots from a double-barreled shotgun, off Prout's Neck.
(Oil, 28¼ x 48½ inches. National Gallery of Art, Washington, D.C. Gift of the Avalon Foundation.)

WINTER
By Rockwell Kent (1882-   ), 1907.
The early paintings done by Rockwell Kent on Monhegan
Island, where he settled in 1905 when he was twenty-three,
are among his finest works.
*(Oil, 33⅞ x 44 inches. The Metropolitan Museum of Art,
New York City. George A. Hearn Fund, 1917).*

THE DORIES
By Charles H. Woodbury (1864-1940).

A long-time resident at Ogunquit, Woodbury pictured the cove there in many different weathers and lights.
(Oil, 30 x 24 inches. Collection of David O. Woodbury.)

Below:
LATE AFTERNOON
By Paul Dougherty (1877-1947), c. 1921.

Monhegan Island is the setting of Dougherty's study of the play of light on foam and rocks.
(Oil, 26½ x 36 inches. Herron Museum of Art, Indianapolis.)

ON THE VERANDAH
By John Singer Sargent (1856-1925), 1921.

Sargent painted his friends the Blaneys—the painter Dwight Blaney, with his wife and two daughters, Margaret and Elizabeth—at their home on Ironbound Island, Frenchman's Bay.
(*Water color, 15 x 20½ inches. Collection of Mr. and Mrs. David Blaney.*)

Opposite:
THE NEXT WAVE
By Frederick Judd Waugh (1861-1940).

Of the painters who "discovered" Maine in the early years
of this century, Waugh was among the most accomplished
and successful.
(Oil, 36 x 38 inches. Herron Museum of Art, Indianapolis.)

PORTRAIT OF THE ARTIST SKETCHING
By John Singer Sargent, 1922.

One of Sargent's least formal and most sympathetic portraits is this one of Dwight Blaney, his friend and host,
sketching on Ironbound Island.
(Oil, 22 x 28 inches. Collection of E. J. Rousuck.)

STORM TIDE
By Robert Henri (1865-1929), 1903.

The scene is Monhegan Island, where Henri and others of the group of young realist painters whose leader he was, began to spend summers in the early 1900s. (*Oil, 26 x 32 inches. Whitney Museum of American Art, New York City.*)

DARK HARBOR FISHERMEN
By N. C. Wyeth (1882-1945).

A noted illustrator, Wyeth did many precise and affectionate paintings of the local fishermen in the Maine places in which he summered.
(*Oil, 30 x 35 inches. Collection of Robert F. Woolworth.*)

MATINICUS
By George W. Bellows (1882-1925), 1916.

Bellows, pupil of Robert Henri, first came to Maine in
1911, and was immediately fascinated by the life of the
island fishermen, as seen here.
(*Oil, 32 x 40 inches. H. V. Allison and Company.*)

IN THE COUNTRY
By Leon Kroll (b. 1884), 1916.

Though not a Henri pupil, Kroll showed his affinity for the new realism in this painting of his friend George Bellows' family, at Camden in 1916.
(*Oil, 46 x 52 inches. Detroit Institute of Arts, Detroit.*)

Below:
TOILERS ON THE SEA
By Rockwell Kent, 1907.

Like his *Winter* (page 106), this painting came out of Kent's early experience on Monhegan Island, ten miles off the coast of Maine.
(*Oil, 38 x 44 inches. New Britain Museum of American Art, New Britain, Connecticut.*)

FISHERMAN'S FAMILY
By George W. Bellows, 1923.

Ten years after his first summer on Monhegan, Bellows painted this reminiscence of
himself, his wife, and first child on the island in 1913.
(*Oil, 37 x 47 inches. Collection of Dr. L. Cabot Briggs.*)

CRIEHAVEN
By George W. Bellows, 1917.

Typical of Bellows is his treatment of the sheen of light on the water, in this painting of the rocky, sheep-pasturing island of Criehaven.
(*Oil, 30 x 44 inches. University of Connecticut, Storrs, Connecticut.*)

in Turner, Maine) had been discussing Emerson's dictum: "Nature being the same on the banks of the Kennebec as on the banks of the Tiber — why go to Europe?" "Bicknell thought that this theory could be pretty well refuted . . . in a certain place he knew of — namely, Turner, Maine. So we went for Turner, Maine." Needless to say, Vedder found there no subjects to compare with Rome, either in landscape or people; but finally "I found in the barn an old pail and some firewood, and made a careful study which I cherish" — and which is now in the Newark Museum. But he had the grace to add that on his later visit to Bowdoin and Bar Harbor, "I found the country beautiful." On the other hand, "In Maine I suffered much from thirst. I found the girls who waited on me at the hotel were superior persons . . . and serious to a degree. This tone I lowered somewhat by asking one of them to bring me apple-pie, — that is, if she had any real *serious* apple-pie."

As cosmopolitanism increased, impressionism, born in France, found its way — rather tardily — to the United States. The old interest in subject matter was replaced by concern for the purely visual aspects of nature — sunlight and shadow, outdoor color, the atmospheric envelopment of objects. A new note of pagan lyricism paralleled society's growing fondness for outdoor life. The summer resort became a favorite painting ground.

A leading pioneer of American impressionism was Childe Hassam, who from the middle 1880s spent many summers in the Isles of Shoals, on Appledore, that peaceful little island frequented by the Boston literati. The sterner wintry aspects of the island, so movingly described by Celia Thaxter, did not attract Hassam; his Appledore was a halcyon world of sunlit gray rocks surrounded by shimmering blue water, with lovely seaside gardens, and girls in white summer dresses. His many Appledore paintings, with their sensitivity to light and outdoor color and soft sea air, their delight in summer by the sea, were among the happiest creations of American impressionism.

It was in Maine that another early impressionist, Willard L. Metcalf, found himself as an artist, during a year on the Damariscotta River, when he developed his characteristic vein of modified impressionism, concerned as much with nature's moods as with visual effects. His was a quiet lyricism, on the verge of sentimentality, yet sometimes, as in "Benediction" (page 100), a moonlit view of an old church at Kennebunkport, summing up the generation's idealistic feeling for the New England past.

The impressionists' sea was a peaceful, sunlit one, devoid of the movement and power of Homer's. But Homer's vigorous realism proved an example to a younger generation of marine painters, most of whom worked for varying periods along the Maine coast. Their favorite theme, like his, was the drama of wave and rock, but their range was more limited (they were primarily specialists) and their viewpoint was more narrowly naturalistic, concerned with literal facts and details, without Homer's largeness of style or strong sense of design. They would have profited by his remark to young Leon Kroll: "Never put more than two waves in a picture; it's fussy." The most accomplished of them was Frederick J. Waugh, an early and frequent visitor to Maine before settling in Provincetown in 1927. His extraordinary technical skill, his mastery of realistic light, color, and motion, his photographic veri-similitude, made him one of the most successful American painters of his time, winner of the popular prize at the Carnegie Institute international exhibitions for five successive years. (Perhaps the good people of Pittsburgh were thus expressing the inlander's longing for the sea.) Charles H. Woodbury, long a resident of Ogunquit, pictured his beloved cove with sensibility to changing weather and light, and a quiet, subtle truthfulness. The younger Paul Dougherty painted the multicolored play of sunlight on foam and rocks with an impressionist brilliance of palette and an unimpressionist energy. To Emil Carlsen, on the other hand, the sea was an ethereal blue and silver expanse, as disembodied as his diaphanous cloud traceries — a highly refined and personal vision, with an element of mysticism.

Allied to these traditionalists in general viewpoint was N. C. Wyeth, famous for his illustrations for *Treasure Island* and countless other books of adventure. For years his summers were spent at Port Clyde and later at Cushing, where he pictured the local fishermen and lobstermen in paintings that combined the illustrator's ability to tell a story with an affectionate, precise portrayal of place and people. This same environment has furnished lifelong material to his gifted son Andrew Wyeth.

Portraiture, which had played so prominent a part in earlier periods, was now mostly in the hands of indigenous artists, who continued the sober, characterful native tradition. But the photograph had begun to compete with the painted portrait; itinerant professionals no longer traveled out of Boston; and, though the well-to-do might visit the metropolis to sit for Tarbell or Benson, the results lacked the vitality of the great days when portraiture was the form of art most in demand by Americans. The brilliant exception was John Singer Sargent, who during his sojourns in Boston visited Maine several times. It was at Ironbound Island that he painted his friend and host, the artist Dwight Blaney, and also the delightful water color, on page 108, of the Blaney family on their veranda. These pictures were Sargent at his least formal — far more sympathetic, both humanly and artistically, than his commissioned portraits of the rich and fashionable. They showed the visual freshness, the infallible eye and unerring hand, that were Sargent's most attractive gifts.

Sculpture on a professional level was still rare. Even more than portraitists, sculptors gravitated toward the large cities, where commissions could be secured; and since Maine had no such cities, her sculptor sons such as Franklin Simmons made their careers elsewhere. Whatever professional sculpture found its way to Maine was the work of sculptors outside the state. Sculpture in America was still largely a matter of the officially commissioned monument or portrait; as an art form independent of such patronage it did not yet exist. Not until our own times have nonacademic sculptors such as Zorach, Lachaise, and Laurent found Maine an ideal place for summer work.

With the opening decade of the twentieth century, the American art world was stirred by the first of the successive revolutions that were to transform it completely. A group of young realist painters, led by Robert Henri, turned from the prevailing academic idealism to frank portrayal of contemporary American life, especially city

116

life. Relishing the native scene in its raw, unsweetened aspects, they abandoned the genteel world of the academy for the broader world of the common man.

While most of the Henri group centered their work on the city, they were by no means confined to it. As early as 1903 Henri was summering and painting on Monhegan Island, ten miles off the Maine coast. With its rock cliffs rising sheer out of deep water as high as a hundred and fifty feet, its magnificent views over miles of open ocean, its fine natural harbor, and its old fishing village whose small year-round population made their living on the sea, Monhegan was rich in pictorial drama.

Henri told his young pupil Rockwell Kent about the island, and in 1905 Kent, just turned twenty-three, settled there for most of the year, building a house with his own hands, and supporting himself by lobstering and carpentry, at the same time painting some of his most original pictures. Though more realistic than his later works, they already revealed Kent's fascination with the wild and remote places of the earth, his admiration for the heroic virtues of their inhabitants, and the mystical strain in his nature, his sense of wonder before the elemental and infinite. These early Monhegan paintings, with their uncompromising clarity, their concentration on the stark forms of the island, and their romantic delight in great expanses of sea, cold northern sky, and brilliant light, were among his most moving works.

It was also through Henri that another brilliant pupil, George Bellows, first visited Monhegan in 1911, and spent the summers of 1913 and 1914 there, followed by two seasons at Ogunquit and Camden. Like Kent, Bellows was enthralled by the hardy life of the island fishermen, as later by the busy shipbuilding world of Camden. But he was concerned less with the monumental forms of the Maine coast than with movement and light: the crash of surf on rocks, the sheen of sunlight on water, the gestures of men working. His keen eye and skilled hand, his gusto in capturing the visual excitement of the world around him, appeared at their purest in these early Maine studies. Several of them were later enlarged into more ambitious, more planned compositions, such as "Fisherman's Family," reproduced on page 113, a reminiscence of his happy life with his wife and first child on Monhegan ten years earlier. Another personal record, but a contemporary one, was his friend Leon Kroll's "In the Country," picturing the Bellows family at Camden in 1916. In this and his many other Maine paintings, Kroll showed his affinity to the new realism (although he was not a Henri student), united to a sensuous idyllicism and an ordered sense of design.

By the second decade of the century, Maine had become a magnet for artists from many other parts of the country, representing many viewpoints, including some of the most advanced of the time. But, as we shall see later, this was only a prelude to the great expansion and diversification of the state's creative life that have taken place in the last fifty years.

— LLOYD GOODRICH

117

The Beginnings
of Modernism,
1914-1940

The Androscoggin, the Kennebec, and the Penobscot flow down to the sea as solemnly as ever, and the numberless inland lakes harbour the loon, and give rest to the angles of geese making south or north according to season, and the black bears roam over the mountain tops as usual.

If the Zeppelin rides the sky at night, and aeroplanes set flocks of sea gulls flying, the gulls remain the same and the rocks, pines, and thrashing seas never lose their power and their native tang.

Nativeness is built of such primitive things, and whatever is one's nativeness, one holds and never loses no matter how far afield the traveling may be.

SO WROTE MARSDEN HARTLEY in 1936, just returned to his native Maine from his own far traveling. But he had not always felt thus. In a letter of 1920 to Kenneth Hayes Miller he had said, "I wonder why I feel so like an alien in New England. . . . I am of polyglot experience if not of blood." Like others in the small band of pioneer American modernists, he had deliberately put behind him his country and its artistic traditions. He had painted abstractions in Berlin, wrestled with Cézanne's concepts of color and form, moved in the revolutionary circles of Paris. Modernism, in the stirring days of its beginning, was strongly cosmopolitan; it was opposed in every respect to the small world of a remote, provincial region. And, indeed, had Hartley not departed, had he not accepted alienation from his past and worked to make the

118

new artistic language of the century his own, he could scarcely have wrought the stark and moving images of Maine which are his crowning achievement.

The venture was necessary, but the price was high: long years of spiritual disorientation and artistic groping. That he truly found himself only after his return to Maine in the last decade of his life is a measure of how necessary, to Hartley at least, were roots in a place — a measure also of how strong a force regionalism (long pronounced dead by most critics) still can be. Perhaps, too, his alienation made more poignant his final return, intensifying the emotion with which he dedicated himself to the rediscovery of his heritage, permitting him to write, with unabashed sentiment, "And so I say to my native continent of Maine, be patient and forgiving, I will soon put my cheek to your cheek, expecting the welcome of the prodigal, and be glad of it, listening all the while to the slow, rich, solemn music of the Androscoggin, as it flows along."

Hartley's experience may stand for that of many others in the great collision that took place in American art early in the present century — a collision between modernism and regionalism, between the new concept of art as a purely aesthetic expression, in which subject matter (if present at all) was of the least importance, and our own long realist tradition, in which subject, rife with associations of time and place, was a vital ingredient. In some parts of America the older concept, especially as it involved regionalism, was virtually demolished in this collision. But not in Maine. There, for reasons that speak eloquently in the art itself, a deep passion for the land, a sense of its unity and of its difference from other lands, a response to its harshness as well as its own singular beauties exerted so constant an influence that no artist working there for any length of time appears to have escaped entirely, while many became, in Hartley's inelegant but expressive word, Maine-iacs.

With some exceptions, Maine's best painters and sculptors in the period covered by this chapter followed a course that paralleled Hartley's to a considerable degree. Early in their careers they were converted to modernism; later they modified their beliefs and altered their art — some more, some less — to express aspects of life which could not be embodied in purely aesthetic terms. Perhaps this modification would have taken place wherever they lived, for the same development occurred widely in America during the 1920s. But the influence of a specific environment seems plainer in the case of Maine than elsewhere. The ways in which it subtly, sometimes profoundly, affected the art of these early modernists is a mark of how important it became in their lives.

Most of them were not born in Maine. They came from Europe and from many parts of the United States. Except for the older Maurice Prendergast, their student days fell roughly in the period from 1905 to 1915, a time of low ebb in American art when the realist tradition, which had culminated in the work of Homer and Eakins appeared to be dying. With few exceptions, they went abroad to study or to paint, usually to Paris. There, during this decade, were Samuel Halpert, Hartley, Bernard Karfiol, Walt Kuhn, Gaston Lachaise, Robert Laurent, John Marin, Waldo Peirce, Prendergast, Maurice Sterne, Abraham Walkowitz, and Marguerite and William Zorach. Almost all were deeply affected by Cézanne, who had already emerged as the old master of modern art. Indeed Prendergast, some ten years before the others arrived, had already built on Cézanne's foundations his own charming art of structured color, which he applied as felicitously to the beach at Ogunquit (page 123) as to Montparnasse.

Many of the younger men went further. These were the days of high excitement when Matisse and the fauves (literally "wild beasts") together with the cubists, led by Braque and Picasso, had just turned the art world upside down and founded the two main movements of modern art — expressionism and abstraction. The Americans joined them, sometimes rather cautiously (like Halpert and Karfiol, who were content with the conservative fauvism of Derain), sometimes embracing one of the more radical trends (as Sterne did cubism), often experimenting (like the Zorachs and Walkowitz) with both fauve and cubist methods. After the Armory Show of 1913, which gave America its first large-scale introduction to modernism, these pioneers were joined by other young Americans who had not been abroad, such as Georgia O'Keeffe, whose abstract drawings were exhibited by Stieglitz in 1916, or Yasuo Kuniyoshi, whose imaginative blend of Oriental and modern art was developed a little later.

And then the student days were over. One by one the young Americans returned to a country still hostile and uncomprehending except for a handful of perceptive critics who understood the aims, the seriousness, and the lasting significance of the revolution which had taken place. One of the latter was Hamilton Easter Field, an indifferent painter but a man of advanced taste who founded and edited *The Arts* magazine, held exhibitions of modern art in his Brooklyn home, befriended many of the young American modernists, and ran a summer art school at Ogunquit, Maine, where they gathered in large numbers — among them Halpert, Hirsch, Karfiol, Kuniyoshi, Laurent, Spencer, Sterne, and Walkowitz. Karfiol's recollections of how he came there are typical. He wrote:

In 1912 . . . Hamilton Easter Field, a new acquaintance, came to Ridgefield [New Jersey] to see my work. He bought a nude, the first sale I had made since 1904. His visit was most encouraging and was followed by an exhibition of my paintings . . . in Field's Brooklyn home. He bought all my pictures in the show. The following summer he invited me to Ogunquit, Maine, where he owned land, houses, and fishing shacks. As he put it, " I want to see what the boys in Ogunquit think of your work." For living quarters he offered me a large one-room shack which served as a fish-house before the Civil War. . . . The view was wonderful through the baton [*sic*] door looking straight out into the cove with colored dories at anchor . . . among the fine rock formations. . . . All my summers since 1914 have been spent there. . . . I never tire of painting Maine.

Thus it was that many of "the boys in Ogunquit" became Maine artists, continuing to work there after Field's death in 1922. Others who arrived by a different route before 1920 were Hopper, Marin, Prendergast, and the Zorachs. During the next dec-

120

ade they were followed by Peter Blume, Lachaise, and O'Keeffe, while Waldo Peirce, born in Bangor, returned in those years to make Maine his permanent home. In the thirties came Ivan Albright and his brother Zsissly; and Hartley returned from his long wanderings.

What happened when the young modernists, fresh from Paris, Munich, and Berlin, came to grips with the physical presence of Maine? One result was the virtual death of abstract art among them. It simply did not lend itself to the expression of a specific locality. Marguerite Zorach made perhaps the bravest attempt to translate her new surroundings into cubist terms. Her "Sailing, Stonington Harbor" of 1919 is a very handsome painting in design but a strangely incongruous one; she must have realized this, for she turned shortly in quite another direction. Maurice Sterne also attempted a fusion of cubism with the Maine scene in a series of rock studies but his success owed much to the inherently cubist structure of his subject, and he, too, moved soon to a more naturalistic style. Hartley and Walkowitz, who had both done some abstract work earlier, were not tempted to revive it for their Maine paintings.

Perhaps it was the group known variously as the immaculates or the precisionists who came closest to applying abstract principles to Maine subjects. Three of them, Stefan Hirsch, Georgia O'Keeffe, and Niles Spencer, worked in the state briefly — none for very long. Seizing on the larger aspects of the landscape, the sweep of sky and sea, the thrust of headland, the boxlike buildings, they simplified these elements into semi-abstract designs which were influenced by cubism but owed at least an equal debt to the native scene. As Spencer put it, writing of "The Cove," which he painted at Ogunquit in 1922, "The contact with the winter scene at this time when the underlying structure of the whole landscape stood out so clearly affected the whole direction of my future work. It left me with the obvious but basic conviction that wherever art ends it begins with nature."

"And returns to nature," many of the young rebels might well have added as they approached their middle years. For the majority of them, grappling with the problems of embodying some aspect of Maine in their art, moved eventually in a more conservative direction. Thus Karfiol, who had used fauvelike distortions of pose and proportion to animate his "Boy Bathers" of 1916, turned by the late twenties to a more sober, more painterly portrayal of landscape and the figure. Samuel Halpert followed a very similar course; his "Rocks, Ogunquit" (page 129) of 1926 is characteristic of the romantic realism which replaced the experimental work of so many artists at this time. Walt Kuhn, too, had painted in various modern idioms around 1920, but like the others abandoned these in favor of a somewhat more rugged naturalism in which the influence of Cézanne long remained apparent, particularly in his still lifes and also perhaps in the strength and monumentality of his figures.

William Zorach traveled an even longer road. Starting as a fauve and cubist painter who was as "wild" as any of the left-bank Americans, and considerably wilder than those above, he became a traditional sculptor and a leading figure in the revival of direct carving — that old and patient process of releasing the image from the block which had been the method of the great sculptural eras of the past only to

121

be half lost in the nineteenth century. No doubt something in Zorach's own nature, which loves tangible and simple things, impelled him in this direction, but Maine, too, played its part, if only in providing the kind of stones he likes, the natural granite boulders whose shapes may suggest a rabbit or a cat and which he often leaves uncut in part, suggesting their original rough contours. Zorach has also relaxed from the painstaking demands of carving by painting quick water colors of the Maine landscape which have the sparkle of genuine spontaneity.

Another Maine sculptor, Robert Laurent, moved from an interest in modern art toward traditional carving in the same years. As his rather mannered early style changed into one of large and simple volumes, the influence of Maine's native folk carvers became briefly apparent. A nude of 1926 (page 131) looks strangely like a cigar-store Indian maiden who has lost her draperies. Maine's third distinguished sculptor in this period was Gaston Lachaise, who summered at Georgetown from 1923 until his death in 1935. Lachaise's most familiar work, the massive women bounded by springing contours of great vitality, derived from the modern French tradition of Maillol and Despiau. This he never relinquished; indeed, he pushed the style toward abstraction in his later years. But his art had another, less familiar aspect which was more intimately connected with his daily life: the penetrating realism of his portraits, with which he caught memorably the eccentric features of his fellow Maine artist, John Marin (page 132).

In the end there was little difference, so far as "modernity" goes, between the work of these artists (except perhaps Lachaise) and those who had not started as modernists but had constantly followed a traditional line. Many of the latter worked in Maine during our period, but one, Edward Hopper, stands out pre-eminently. Though Hopper had been at Ogunquit and Monhegan before 1920, his finest Maine work was done in the summers of 1926, 1927, and 1929, when he painted at Rockland and Cape Elizabeth. Coming out of the Homer tradition of vigorous naturalism, painterly technique, and the bold handling of light and atmosphere, Hopper added his own note of austerity and loneliness, singularly appropriate to the aspects of Maine which appealed to him. Among these were its isolated lighthouses on their barren headlands, the character and solidity of its Victorian architecture, seen in his "Libby House, Portland" (page 134), the dusty commonplaceness of its back-country roads. What a different Maine it is from the warm life of children, barns, and family activities depicted by Waldo Peirce, another traditionalist who found in the vivacity of French impressionism a style just as appropriate to his own vision.

But in the long run it was neither the traditionalists nor the modernists-turned-traditional who created the most intense distillation of Maine in these years. Rather, it was two men, Marsden Hartley and John Marin, who never gave up their search for a modern idiom and who succeeded in making it the vehicle for what they felt for the land. Both were expressionists, and expressionism may be roughly defined as the radical distortion of natural forms and the free or arbitrary use of color to express emotion. But it is more an attitude than a style, and nothing could have been more different than its use by Hartley and Marin or the visions of Maine which they projected.

THE STONY BEACH, OGUNQUIT
By Maurice Prendergast (1861-1924), 1901.
Building on Cézanne's foundations, Prendergast applied
his own art of structured color to Maine subjects as he had
to Parisian.
*(Water color, 20¾ x 13½ inches. Collection of Dr. and
Mrs. MacKinley Helm.)*

MOVEMENT, SEA AND SKY
By John Marin (1870-1953), 1946.

"This day is a peach," Marin wrote, "clear and snappy, the tide is in, the water a crystal green, the sky coming down to the waters, indescribable brilliancy." These are the qualities of Maine that so often inform Marin's art.

(Oil, 22 x 28 inches. Collection of the William H. Lane Foundation. Courtesy of the Downtown Gallery, New York City.)

SAILING, STONINGTON HARBOR
By Marguerite Zorach (1887-   ), 1919.

One of the earliest to attempt to combine cubist design with Maine subject matter, Marguerite Zorach soon turned in another direction.
(*Oil, 25 x 30 inches. Collection of the artist.*)

ROCKY CLIFFS
By Maurice Sterne (1878-1957), 1915-1917.

The inherent structure of the rocks Sterne took as his subject aided him in his efforts to fuse the cubist method with the Maine scene.
(*Drawing, 22 x 16½ inches. Bixler Art and Music Center, Colby College, Waterville. Gift of Mr. and Mrs. Sidney Simon.*)

OGUNQUIT, MAINE:
OLD HOME
By Abraham Walkowitz
(1880-   ), 1926.

*(Oil, 26 x 40 inches. Collection
of Dr. Rosa E. Prigosen.)*

THE COVE
By Niles Spencer (1893-1952),
1922.

*(Oil, 28 x 36 inches. Newark
Museum, Newark, New Jersey.)*

COURTHOUSE,
ALFRED, MAINE
By Stefan Hirsch (1899-   ).

*(Casein, 32 x 41 inches. Collec-
tion of Mr. and Mrs. Robert
Laurent.)*

The work of the Immaculates, or Precisionists—a group that included Georgia O'Keeffe, Niles Spencer, and Stefan Hirsch—simplified the larger aspects of the Maine landscape into semi-abstract designs, influenced by cubism but reflecting equally the actual forms of the native scene.

WAVE, NIGHT
By Georgia O'Keeffe (1887-   ), 1928.
(*Oil, 30 x 36 inches. Addison Gallery of American Art, Phillips Academy, Andover, Massachusetts. Gift of Charles L. Stillman.*)

BREAKFAST IN THE BARN
By Waldo Peirce (1884-   ), 1939.

(Oil, 40 x 50 inches. Midtown Galleries, New York City.)

Fauve distortions of proportion and pose were used by Karfiol in his *Boy Bathers*, while Peirce found his inspiration in the more conservative tradition of French impressionism.

ROCKS, OGUNQUIT
By Samuel Halpert (1884-1930), 1926.

Like other artists in the late 1920s, Halpert turned away from the experimental toward a romantic realism, as seen here. (*Oil. Collection of Gerald Gewirtz.*)

Opposite:
BOY BATHERS
By Bernard Karfiol (1886-1952), 1916.

(*Oil, 28 x 36 inches. Whitney Museum of American Art, New York City.*)

KANSAS, PORTRAIT OF THE
ARTIST AS A CLOWN
By Walt Kuhn (1880-1943), 1932.

The influence of Cézanne remained apparent in the monumentality of the naturalistic figures Kuhn painted after he abandoned the modernism of the twenties. (*Oil, 31½ x 21½ inches. Broadmoor Hotel, Colorado Springs, Colorado.*)

WILLIAM ZORACH (1887-   )

(*Right*) THE COVE, 1927
(*Water color, 14⅞ x 21⅞ inches. Mr.
and Mrs. Frank G. Logan Collection,
Art Institute of Chicago.*)

(*Below*) RECLINING CAT, 1935
(*Granite boulder, 11 inches high x 16
inches long. Downtown Gallery, New
York City.*)

Opposite:
YOUNG GIRL
By Robert Laurent (1890-   ), 1926.

(*Teak, 7 x 18 x 54 inches. Museum of Art of Ogunquit.
Gift of Henry Strater.*)

130

GASTON LACHAISE (1882-1935) HEAD OF JOHN MARIN, 1928 (Museum of Fine Arts, Boston.)

GASTON LACHAISE (1882-1935) FEMALE TORSO *(Museum of Art, Ogunquit.)*

Above: RAILROAD CROSSING, 1926
(Water color, 14 x 20 inches. Collection of Mr. and Mrs. Herbert Goldstone.)

THE MAINE OF EDWARD HOPPER (1882-   )

Below: LIBBY HOUSE, PORTLAND, 1927
(Water color, 14 x 20 inches. Fogg Art Museum, Harvard University, Cambridge, Massachusetts.)

MAINE COAST
By Peter Blume (1906-   ), 1926.   135

Blume employs realistic elements to create startling images, as in
this semi-primitive vision of a Maine scene.
(*Oil, 30 x 40 inches. Collection of Mr. and Mrs. R. Sturgis Ingersoll.*)

MAINE ISLANDS, 1922
*(Water color, 16¾ x 20 inches. Phillips Collection, Wash-
ington, D.C.)*

Opposite:
TREE AND SEA, MAINE, 1919
*(Water color, 13⅝ x 16½ inches. Alfred Stieglitz Collec-
tion, Art Institute of Chicago.)*

136

137

YASUO KUNIYOSHI (1893-1953)

Right:
THE SWIMMER, 1924
*(Oil, 20⅛ x 30⅛ inches. Ferdinand Howald Collection,
Columbus Gallery of Fine Arts, Columbus, Ohio.)*

Below:
MAINE FAMILY c. 1922
(Oil, 30 x 24 inches. Phillips Collection, Washington, D.C.)

Kuniyoshi: "I have practised starting my work from reality, stating the facts before me. Then I paint without the object . . . combining reality and imagination."

Opposite:
AH GOD, HERRINGS, BUOYS —
THE GLITTERING SEA
By Ivan Albright (1897-   ), 1940.

For Albright, "A painting is life and a painting is death, both making and lying in the coffin built for tomorrow's use."
(Oil, 30³⁄₁₆ x 38 inches. Collection of the artist.)

THE WAVE, 1940
(Oil on fiber board, 30¼ x 40⅞ inches. Worcester Art Museum, Worcester, Massachusetts.)

THREE STUDIES OF MAINE BY MARSDEN HARTLEY (1877-1943)

GIVE US THIS DAY, 1938-1939
(Oil, 30 x 40 inches. Collection of Ione and Hudson D. Walker.)

140

MT. KATAHDIN, AUTUMN, No. 1, 1939-1940
Hartley: "Whatever is one's nativeness, one holds and
never loses no matter how far afield the traveling may be."
*(Oil, 30⅛ x 40 inches. F. M. Hall Collection, University
of Nebraska Art Galleries, Lincoln, Nebraska.)*

LIGHTHOUSE AT TWO LIGHTS
By Edward Hopper, 1929.
The note of austerity and loneliness which Hopper added
to the naturalistic tradition within which he painted was
appropriate to those aspects of Maine that appealed to him.
(*Oil, 29 x 43 inches. The Metropolitan Museum of Art,
New York City, Hugo Kastor Fund, 1962.*)

Just as Hartley wrote that "nativeness is built of such primitive things" as rocks and gulls, sea and mountain, so in his painting he gave them an equally primitive character — rugged, bare, simplified to the point of woodenness. A wave is frozen eternally in its upflung gesture against a wall of rock; it will never crash, recede, ebb, or flow, like the watery waves of Waugh; it stands as a symbol, rather than an illusion, of the sea's might. Mt. Katahdin, like the clouds around it, is more carved than painted; the harsh contrasts of form and color build a static pattern wonderfully expressive of Hartley's response to the wildness and strength of the landscape. The formal design of gulls and fish in "Give Us This Day" (page 140), together with the deliberate dislocations of scale and perspective, suggest a ritual of survival on the harsh shore, not an event observed. The Maine that emerges from Hartley's painting is a land of enduring, majestic strength, a rock in both the physical and spiritual sense.

Marin's Maine is not without these qualities, but it is less primitive, more vivacious. "This day is a peach," he wrote Stieglitz in 1923, "clear and snappy, the tide is in, the water a crystal green, the sky coming down to the waters, indescribable brilliancy. The boats dance. Everything is dancing. To Hell with Gloom. Even my boat feels the day. It has a jump on it." He painted as he wrote, with an ecstatic and staccato energy. The word "movement" recurs often in his titles. Here is no frozen sea, no graven clouds, but a constantly flowing, clashing, dancing play of forces. Even his islands refuse to stay still; they sail like battleships across the paper. A tree is recognizably a pine, but it is also an explosion — an explosion in form and an explosion of Marin's intense feeling for the vitality he sensed in everything around him.

Stylistically, Marin owed much to Cézanne and the cubists, as his breaking of planes and his apparently arbitrary compartmenting of space indicates. But there was nothing truly arbitrary or abstract in his method; it was intimately, indeed fiercely related to what he saw and felt. "I don't paint rocks, trees, houses, and all things seen, I paint an inner vision. Rubbish. If you have an intense love and feeling towards these things, you'll try your damndest to put on paper or canvas that thing. You can transpose, you can play with and on your material, but when you are finished that's got to have the roots of that thing in it and no other thing." Marin's Maine was as strong as Hartley's, but, like his boat, it jumped with life.

After the veterans of modernism came a younger generation of artists, who brought to Maine some of the many directions which American art was beginning to explore. Among these was a vein of fantasy approaching surrealism, although none of the three men discussed below could be called orthodox surrealists. In part, they were the product of that liberation from strict fidelity to nature which modernism offered. They also took from various modern movements the quality of surprise, of the visually unexpected. This they used, according to their various natures, to create startling images which reveal less of Maine than of their own humorous, odd, or macabre way of seeing things.

Of the three, the Japanese-born Yasuo Kuniyoshi was the oldest, straddling generations, as it were. Field had brought him to Ogunquit as a young art student in

1918, and it was there, a few years later, that he painted a series of highly individual pictures in which he combined elements of modern and Oriental art in sprightly designs full of sly humor. Sometimes these were closely related to his observations; "Maine Family" (page 138) catches the essence of rural respectability at the same time that it gives one the peculiar sensation of seeing a familiar scene through the eyes of an alien culture. At other times he fabricated purely fantastic, dreamlike images, such as an incredibly buoyant swimmer floating in a dark sea toward a lighthouse impossibly large for its distance. This is nobody's Maine but Kuniyoshi's. And, different as it is, one might say almost the same things of Peter Blume's "Maine Coast" (page 135), for here too is an enigmatic situation: a naked woman holding a dog, a man at the door, a grotesquely large face peering out the window. In spite of its greater realism in certain details, such as the house, here also are a decorative patterning in the figures and silhouette of trees against the sky, a semi-primitive vision, and a delight in the incongruous.

Last of the three to arrive in Maine was Ivan Le Lorraine Albright, who spent the summers of 1939 to 1941 in the neighborhood of Corea. Albright's fantasy, if one can call it that, was not the result of ignoring realism but of pushing it far beyond its normal scope (although it might be argued that this too is a liberation from its conventional bounds). In any case, Albright's work has a strangeness that comes partly from the microscopic detail with which every object is painted, partly from the aura of death and imminent decay which pervades his pictures, with their long, biblical-sounding titles — such as "Ah God, Herrings, Buoys — the Glittering Sea" (page 139). At first glance only a still-life arrangement of commonplace objects, this is a painting that grows into a comment on the transitory nature of life, and, in some mysterious manner (perhaps through the iridescent color) a revelation of the beauty in death.

And so modernism, or at least certain aspects of it, came to Maine as it came to other parts of the country, profoundly altering the traditional ways of seeing, drawing, painting, carving. But Maine itself, as Hartley foresaw, proved indestructible. It put on the artist the burden of reconciling his new vision with his old love. Faced with this challenge, some met it head on, some went back to an older tradition, but not one turned his back totally on the land to devote himself to purely aesthetic problems. Regionalism, in the best, not the chauvinistic sense of the word, survived in Maine as it scarcely did elsewhere. It nurtured an art rooted in love and spiritual need — an art, in Hartley's words again, of "heraldic images to be genuflective offerings to place."

— JOHN I. H. BAUR

The quotations from Marsden Hartley are from his essay, "On the Subject of Nativeness—a Tribute to Maine" (catalogue of Hartley exhibition, An American Place, 1937), and from an unpublished letter in the possession of the Whitney Museum of American Art. Karfiol's description of Ogunquit is from his foreword to *Bernard Karfiol*, American Artists Group, 1945. The quotation from Niles Spencer is from *A Museum in Action*, Newark Museum, 1944. All the Marin quotations are from *The Selected Writings of John Marin*, edited by Dorothy Norman, 1949. The quotations from Albright and Kuniyoshi are from *New Art in America*, edited by John I. H. Baur, 1957.

144

The Diversity
of Our Time,
1940-1963

IN OUR TIME THE SAME FORCES which drew artists to Maine in the past are still in effect: the land and sea, which are unchanged and for the most part unchangeable, and the opportunity for solitude in which one's thoughts can evolve at their intended pace. If we wished to find the artists themselves, we would, therefore, go to sparsely populated places that are difficult to find, where the most evident thing is the presence of nature. But their works are what interest us, and those gathered together here demonstrate that the stimulus of Maine is still as strong in the period from 1940 to the present as ever before.

The difference between the present and the past is that now there is not only a greater number of paintings and sculptures which qualify for inclusion in a book or exhibition of Maine art, but also a much greater diversity. Anyone who considers the art of our time — in the world, in the United States, or in Maine — will find a vast range of styles and methods. There is no use in looking for the simple unanimity of a century ago when the only noticeable difference among artists working in Maine was their sophistication or their naïveté, depending on whether they had been trained in the cities or the "provinces." In either case they shared an interest in people, places, and things. The contemporary artist has, for the most part, less kinship of interests in the visible world because he is engaged more with looking inward than outward, and in this inner world he finds the great diversity which he records.

This looking inward has produced a present-day art of painting which is characteristically non-objective and often identifiable as "abstract expressionism" or "action painting." Its sculptural counterpart, embracing the "found object" and the "assemblage," also proclaims the forces which produced it: human action intensified by the welding torch or, in extreme cases, the pile driver. This frequently rough-shod art represents in our time a kind of wide-eyed rediscovery of the will. We shall find some of it in art from Maine just as we should in the other forty-nine states. But there is less than in many parts of our world simply because so many Maine artists want to look outward as well as inward. The impact of the place on the artist is as strong as ever, although it now finds other avenues of expression.

The best known of America's outward-looking artists, Andrew Wyeth, spends half of his year in Maine. As a youthful painter in the late 1930s and early 1940s he produced many brilliant water colors which caught the drama and excitement of wind, waves, and sunlight, and the actions of men living in the Maine environment. Aware of the danger of being dominated by the easy effects of the medium, he began to do more sustained water-color studies like the one of Broad Cove Farm shown on page 154, and soon turned to the medium of egg tempera. This change in medium accompanied a deepening of feeling in his more mature work.

"Northern Point" and "Wind from the Sea" are two of the highly finished tempera paintings in which Wyeth brings to our attention combinations of things no one had noticed before him. Both natural forms and man-made objects enter into these combinations, each of which is unique. The elements in "Northern Point" are few but concentrated; the lightning rod with its tactile appeal is seen against the least tactile of substances, fog, in a juxtaposition that is quiet but evocative. Visual reality is transcended in the close rendering of surfaces, near and far. In "Wind from the Sea" the distance becomes silhouette and the foreground closely observed texture, while sunlight, shadow, and wind bring outdoors and indoors together. The romantic aspect one feels in these paintings relates them to much American art of the past and, for those who know Maine's coast and the houses near it, an appeal to sentiment is especially felt. This is no affectation on Wyeth's part, for he and his family live in a modest, simply furnished, early American house at the edge of the sea.

From this extreme of detailed naturalism we turn to the opposite pole — the highly abstract paintings of William Kienbusch. While representing an opposite philosophy, Kienbusch still retains a contact — even a close contact — with the world of visual experience. If we run through the titles of his works — "Pines after Snowstorm," "The Red Buoy," "Island Wreck," "Ocean in the Apple Tree," or the one reproduced in these pages, "Sea Grass," it is brought to our attention how directly the artist draws his material from nature. Looking at the pictures which bear these titles, we quite clearly sense the image in each, though the artist's inward looking has strongly modified what the camera would record. (It is interesting that he does use a camera to bring home the record of a scene, while Wyeth never does.)

In "Sea Grass" there are not many things which are individually recognizable, but the total bears a relation to the complex of grass and water and light. It is characteristic of Kienbusch that he distills everything to its simplest terms and that he

146

combines apparently automatic strokes of the brush with extremely sensitive choices of color. Eight years before, in "Backyard, Winter, Maine," when lines and rectangular composing were common in his work, he was more concerned with separate objects and the sense of a total space. But in this earlier work he was also concerned with distilling out highly selected qualities in the scene.

In the way in which his art is inextricably linked with the Maine scene, Kienbusch is typical of the "abstract" artists working in Maine today. Though they may bear a resemblance to members of the "New York school," they differ from them in having affection for a land and seascape which provide their thematic material. There is less impersonalism in their art, and none are real "non-objectivists." William Kienbusch is typical again in that he found himself as an artist in Maine. "I was born and brought up in New York City," he has said, "and it has always been somewhat of a surprise and mystery to me that my strongest creative feelings are concerned with the New England and Maine landscapes. The summers of 1940 and 1941 at Stonington on Deer Isle were the decisive ones."

Wyeth and Kienbusch are representatives of extremes; there also are many in-between currents in the stream of Maine art during the decades of the forties and fifties. Some of these are a continuation of what we saw in the previous decades, notably in the work of those artists whose careers span both periods. Among these, two sculptors stand out.

It was a happy occasion when the city of Bath, in August 1962, unveiled the fountain which is William Zorach's gift to the Maine community with which he has been closely associated for many years. "The Spirit of the Sea," as it is called, expresses also the spirit of youth and is a fitting climax to forty years of work in Maine. It comes as an extra dividend that William Zorach is also one of the best water colorists in the state, carrying on an interest we saw in an earlier period.

At Cape Neddick, near Ogunquit, another major American sculptor continues to produce works, some of which are directly inspired by the sea. Robert Laurent's "Tuna," page 156, reflects this artist's willingness to experiment with newer sculptural forms as he transforms the massive strength of the fish into its equivalent in tense bronze bands. Like Zorach, Laurent has spent summers in Maine for forty years; in the winters he has been, until his recent retirement, professor of sculpture at the University of Indiana.

Also associated for a long time with Ogunquit is a painter who has done a great deal to share his love and knowledge of art with others. Henry Strater, as well as being the author of solidly painted landscape, figure, and still-life paintings such as "Lobster on Black Tray," shown on page 157, has been director of the Museum of Art of Ogunquit and has supervised its active summer program during the ten years of its existence. His influence on art in Maine extends back as far as 1919 and will be felt long into the future.

Marguerite Zorach carries on her painting with continued freshness of approach. Her most recent paintings tend to be more naturalistic, with less of the stylization deriving from European art than earlier in her career. There are strong, simplified shapes but, generally speaking, a love of nature has won out over stylization, much as it has in her husband's art. Their daughter, Dahlov Ipcar, has also attained a position of note among Maine artists. Animals of all kinds are her chief subject matter, sometimes isolated for the graceful patterns they create, and sometimes seen in the context of a familiar Maine setting.

Two other artists of the generation of the Zorachs and Robert Laurent who are still important American painters are Waldo Peirce and Henry Varnum Poor. Waldo Peirce, who seems to have discovered the fountain of youth, today produces pictures which are as sure in touch and as sensitive in color as the works of his first youth mentioned in the previous chapter.

Henry Varnum Poor came to Maine after the war to join the faculty of the newly formed Skowhegan School of Painting and Sculpture. As a teacher (and as president of the school) he has had an effect on American art beyond that of his own painting, but it is the latter which interests us here. Over the last seventeen years the landscape of Maine has become more and more germane to his art. "Between Summer and Autumn" indicates the degree to which this artist, who has been well known as a painter and ceramic designer for decades, has combined a mastery of drawing, a sensitive feeling for paint, and a fresh approach to the seeing of nature into a style that is traditional but yet looks new.

Among the artists of an older generation who made a considerable contribution to Maine art during the forties and early fifties is Carl Sprinchorn. His work has brought forth praise from, among others, Marsden Hartley, who in an unpublished article said, "When I look at these pictures I see my native land pictured with such speaking accuracy that I feel almost as if they had been done for me and I glory in their vividness and veracity." Sprinchorn's masculinity found sympathetic subject matter in the Maine woods and its lumbermen. He sees the men and their setting in analogous, forceful shapes, and his color is exciting in the way that white snow, dark green trees, and warm-tinted winter brush can be.

Living another kind of life of retirement from the world was Herman Roessler, who, as a recluse in China, Maine, was brought to public attention only after his death in 1955. Many of his hauntingly imaginative colored drawings and occasional paintings are preserved in the Boston Museum of Fine Arts.

Spectacular Monhegan Island still exerts its spell over artists who continue in the tradition of Bellows and Henri. Jay Connaway has produced probably the most powerful transcriptions of the crashing wave among the more conservative group of artists. Andrew Winter, until his death in 1958, was among the best loved, as man and as artist, of those who inhabited Monhegan. He and Connaway both spent many rugged winters on the island and recorded them in strong pictures.

Among the artists whose studies of Monhegan began to result in more modern-looking paintings during the 1940s was Ernest Fiene. Joseph de Martini is a resident of many years whose paintings are a successful modification of a conservative interest by a modern emphasis on strong textures and shapes. At the present time he is the dean of Monhegan artists, with such men as Ernest Hekking and Leo Meissner producing solid paintings in a similar vein. Meanwhile, a newer generation continues the sixty-year-old tradition of painting on Monhegan, and of some of these we will speak later.

The three currents we have touched upon: detailed naturalism, near abstraction, and the persistence of older traditions, may now be explored with further examples and with attention to the interrelationships which reveal the richness of the art of today.

While Wyeth produces the most evocative painting in the sharply realistic manner, there are others who work in this general way with great intensity, each with his unmistakable touch. Malvin Albright (brother of Ivan Albright), who paints under the name of Zsissly, has, over the last twenty-five years, recorded scenes of Pemaquid, Boothbay, and Corea, where he now spends his summers. "Boothbay Harbor, Maine" is characteristic of his many coastal scenes which combine precision with intensity of feeling. Precision and expert craftsmanship are basic to the art of Stow Wengenroth also. Lithography is his chosen medium, and it suits well his transcriptions of Maine's buildings, landscape, and wildlife.

Thomas Fransioli has painted Maine for many years. While he now concentrates on harbor scenes, the painting of 1948, "The Way to Penobscot," reproduced on page 161, in its clear-cut fixation on the objects is surprisingly like Jonathan Fisher's "View of Bluehill" of 1824 (see page 43). Shadows are sharp-edged and decorative, and their arbitrariness is in contrast to the more literal treatment found in the paintings of John Chumley. Both artists work in a frankly nostalgic vein. Another sharp-seeing painter, Stephen Etnier, has a less ideal vision. He frequently contrasts the litter of man with the sublimity of sky and sea, the picturesque effect of the whole bringing about a harmony between them.

Ever since Winslow Homer demonstrated that the most luminous effects in painting could be achieved in the medium of water color, New England has been a center of this art form. There are today many good water colorists at work in Maine — too many to do justice to here — but, in addition to Wyeth and Zorach, two of the professionals should be singled out. James Elliott of West Bath and Vincent Hartgen of Orono and the University of Maine both concentrate on nature without evidence of man, and both find their effects in waves, rocks, and trees, using expert technique to record them. There the similarity ends, since Hartgen's interests are basically expressionistic while Elliott's are basically naturalistic. A distinct personality among water colorists is Susie Thompson, a friend of John Marin during his lifetime, whose feminine touch modifies a conservative version of Marin's style.

Turning to the more abstract artists who are a major force in our art, we find that, like Kienbusch, they are all concerned with expressing aspects of the natural world within a language that is essentially abstract. John Heliker's development toward increased abstraction is an interesting one. His works of ten or fifteen years ago are strongly sculptural in their chunky interpretations of coastal forms. By the mid 1950s he had arrived at the interplay of faceted planes and lines that we see in "Bridge at Stonington." Color gradually becomes a greater force for synthesis right up to his work of the present time, in which the search for fusion in pictorial terms has subordinated the tactile existence of objects. But these are not lost; the character of rocks is differentiated from that of trees, while the sense of flickering light passing over everything is almost lyrical.

Reuben Tam uses the strong impact of rich textured paint to express very directly and with a minimum of factual data the things that he feels about the sea and coast. Of all the younger men who have chosen to paint Monhegan Island, he has perhaps come forward with the most original manner of treating the old themes. Instead of a static view, which inevitably emphasizes the objects of nature, he is after less tangible effects, which are hinted at in some titles: "Shores of Light," "Fault and Weathering," "The Salt Sea," the last of which he describes as being "about glint and glare, surge, edges, and all the other marks by which one memorizes the sea over the years."

There are other men of the new generation at work on Monhegan, and each summer brings new artists, some of whom will stay. For bold, simplified pictures, made up of abstracted shapes suggested by the island, we would single out Hans Moller, a European-trained artist who has recently become a summer resident. And back on shore, David von Schlegell and Edward Betts at Ogunquit have found evocative ways of characterizing the ruggedness of the Maine coast in near-abstractions.

From a winter residence in San Francisco, Jason Schoener comes each summer to his Maine home on Georgetown Island. Light playing on water, rocks, and trees is at the core of his art. He arrived at the degree of abstraction we see in "Lunar Tide," (page 163) by evolution from a more realistic water-color style, and if we could see a sequence of his works we could follow his growing interest in the less tangible aspects of nature, recorded as a kind of fusion of impressions.

John Muench of South Freeport is the director of the Portland School of Fine and Applied Art and a nationally known print maker. His paintings, of increasing importance in his output, verge on the completely abstract sometimes, but more often deal with the forces of nature and the ways in which these can be symbolized with color and paint. Also a print maker, as well as a painter, is Karl Schrag, who has worked at Sprucehead Island, Friendship, and Deer Isle. He sees nature in linear rather than painterly terms, partly because of his association with Stanley Hayter and his Atelier 17, and finds his inspiration almost wholly in the rhythms of grasses and water. Rhythms, too, and the sense of motion they convey, pervade the paintings of Miss Denny Winters of Rockport.

Bernard Langlais has recently turned from painting to the making of montage-like constructions from chunks of wood. "Last Train Up River" incorporates a humorous touch into a work which reveals a feeling for shape, color, and texture within the range prescribed by this material. If his constructions are close to relief sculpture, the montages of Miss Mildred Burrage of Wiscasset are closer to painting. The sheets of mica she uses in these reveal their local and natural origin as the wood used by Langlais does. For more about Miss Burrage the reader is referred to the section of this book dealing with galleries in Maine, for in her sponsorship of two galleries of contemporary art and several historical museums she and her sister have done an immeasurable service for the people and the artists of Maine.

WIND FROM THE SEA
By Andrew Wyeth (1917-   ), 1947.
The house pictured here belonged to Christina Olson, the
subject of the well-known *Christina's World*. The artist
tells of going into an upstairs room which had been closed
off for years. Then: "I opened the window and this is
what happened."
*(Tempera, 18½ x 27½ inches. Collection of Mr. and Mrs.
Charles H. Morgan.)*

ROCKS AND TREES
By John Heliker (1909-   ), 1961.
The strokes here have nearly the freedom
of the "action" painter's, yet they are
directed by what the artist has seen in
nature.
*(Oil, 50 x 40 inches. Whitney Museum
of American Art, New York City. Gift
under the Ford Foundation Purchase
Program.)*

Below:
SEAGRASS
By William Kienbusch
(1914-   ), 1962
In the eight years since painting "Backyard, Winter" *(opposite)*, Kienbusch has
adopted a freer brush stroke and has
turned away from man-made objects as
sources for his near-abstractions.
*(Oil, 32 x 41 inches. Kraushaar Galleries,
New York City.)*

BACKYARD, WINTER, MAINE
By William Kienbusch, 1954.

In his selection of different strokes to stand for different
objects, Kienbusch reminds us of the Oriental painter.
(*Casein, 27 x 36 inches. Collection of Mrs. Gertrude H.
Moore.*)

153

Left:
BETWEEN SUMMER AND
AUTUMN
By Henry Varnum Poor (1888-   ),
1960.

The sympathy we feel here with the forms
and movements of trees is the outcome
of hundreds of studies done near the artist's farmhouse, near Lakewood.
(*Oil, 43 x 47 inches. Rehn Gallery, New
York City.*)

Opposite:
NORTHERN POINT
By Andrew Wyeth, 1950.

Subjects from the region around Port
Clyde and Cushing have appeared in Wyeth's work for more than twenty years.
(*Oil, 36 x 18³⁄₁₆ inches. Wadsworth Athe-
neum, Hartford, Connecticut.*)

BROAD COVE FARM
By Andrew Wyeth, 1940.

Done at the same time as his more rapid water colors, this
sustained painting anticipates Wyeth's work in tempera.
(*Water color, 28 x 40 inches. Portland Museum of Art,
Portland.*)

TUNA
By Robert Laurent.

The lighter, more open treatment of the great fish in this recent work is in contrast with the style of Laurent's earlier sculpture (as on page 131).
(*Bronze, 16 x 38 inches. Collection of the artist.*)

MARGUERITES
By Waldo Peirce, 1962.

Joyful feelings associated with summers in Maine have continued to find expression in Waldo Peirce's art.
(*Oil, 30 x 24 inches. Midtown Galleries, New York City.*)

BROOK IN SNOW
By Marguerite Zorach, c. 1953.

While reading geometry into the forms of rocks and snow here, the artist does not interrupt natural sequences with cubist abstraction as in her earlier work (see page 125).
(*Oil, 28 x 22 inches. Collection of the artist.*)

LOBSTER ON BLACK TRAY
By Henry Strater (1896-   ), 1960.

The simplified areas of color and broad handling of oil paint are constants in Henry Strater's art.
(*Oil, 18 x 24 inches. Rehn Gallery, New York City.*)

157

Right:
BOOTHBAY HARBOR, MAINE
By Zsissly (Malvin Marr Albright) (1897-   )

A dedicated and craftsmanlike transcription of nature is found in this view of one of Maine's most popular harbors. *(Oil, 24 x 48 inches. Collection of the artist.)*

Below:
ON THE FLATS
By Stephen Etnier (1903-   ), 1959.

Etnier is a year-round resident of South Harpswell and a veteran painter of the coast. Like most of today's sharp realists, he prefers the sea quiet rather than turbulent. *(Oil, 15 x 34 inches. Milch Gallery, New York City.)*

Bottom:
THREE SWINGS
By John Chumley (1928-   ), 1961.

Through his variety of soft and sharp edges this artist explores the range of sunlight effects. *(Oil, 30 x 40 inches. Collection of Mr. and Mrs. Peter F. Carleton.)*

LOBSTER SHACKS, MONHEGAN ISLAND
By Ernest Fiene (1894-   ), 1951.

Among other things the artist is concerned here with the
balance between the use of textures to identify the object
and their use to create a paint surface.
(*Oil, 28 x 32 inches. Midtown Galleries, New York City.*)

THE SPECTATOR
By Carl Sprinchorn (1887-   ), 1949.

This painting was done at Shin Pond in the Katahdin region, where the artist lived three years among the woodsmen.
(Oil, 28 x 34 inches. Collection of the artist.)

PRESIDENT J. SEELYE BIXLER
OF COLBY COLLEGE
By Willard W. Cummings (1915-   ), 1959.

During Dr. Bixler's presidency the college completed its move to Mayflower Hill in Waterville and made great advances academically. He founded the departments of art and music, which are now housed in a new building bearing his name. Willard Cummings has also had a close interest in the artistic life of Colby College.
(Oil, 50 x 36 inches. Colby College.)

THE WAY TO PENOBSCOT
By Thomas Fransioli (1906-   ), 1948.

The decorative blends with the naturalistic in the paintings
of Thomas Fransioli.
(*Oil, 30 x 42 inches. Collection of Joseph Lasser.*)

**BLACKSMITH TENT,
TOPSHAM FAIR**
By Dahlov Ipcar (1917-   ), 1939.

The limber curves of the trotting horse
are echoed throughout this painting.
(*Oil, 25 x 40 inches. Colby College.*)

161

BRIDGE AT STONINGTON
By John Heliker, 1956.

This phase of the artist's career is halfway between his earlier, sculptural manner and the fusion of form with light seen in his most recent work.
(*Oil, 14⅞ x 20 inches. Collection of Mary C. Miller.*)

Below:
LUNAR TIDE
By Jason Schoener (1919-   ), 1960.

The merging of the "seen" and the "felt" here is typical of a number of artists who are working in Maine today.
(*Oil, 44 x 60 inches. Midtown Galleries, New York City.*)

Opposite, top:
STEAMED CLAMS
By John Laurent (1921-   ), 1961.

John Laurent is among those artists who are today returning to a more representational style.
(*Oil, 36¼ x 20 inches. Collection of Christopher L. Huntington.*)

Opposite, bottom:
LAST TRAIN UP RIVER
By Bernard Langlais (1924-   ), 1959.

A native of Old Town, Langlais served his first apprenticeship with his father, a carpenter.
(*Wood, 23 x 29 inches. Pace Gallery, Boston.*)

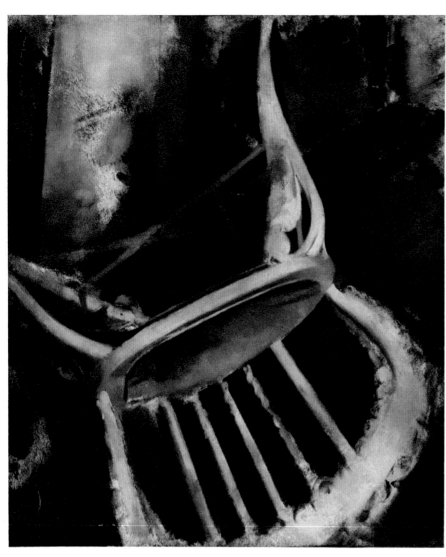

THE CHAIR
By Edwin Dickinson (1891-   ), 1956.

Dickinson's combining of subtle realistic representation and intriguingly unreal situations has brought him widespread recognition in recent years.
(*Oil on masonite, 12 x 15 inches. Collection of Mr. and Mrs. Herbert A. Goldstone.*)

UNTITLED
By Alex Katz (1927-   ), 1961.

A quick visual impression seems to be the starting point of many of this artist's paintings. The image, in almost flat colors, is then locked into the rectangle of the picture.
(*Oil, 49½ x 50 inches. Stable Gallery, New York City.*)

164

STORM LEDGE
By John Muench (1914-   ), 1961.

While the first impact of this picture is of
bold color shapes, there is no doubt of
its origin in the sea breaking over rocks.
(*Oil, 36 x 47 inches. Collection of James
B. Ross.*)

Below:

TOP OF THE BLUFF
By Fairfield Porter (1907-   ), 1961.

In choosing subjects of potential senti-
mental interest and treating them in a
detached and moderately formalized way,
Porter resembles the masters of French
Impressionism.
(*Oil, 36 x 36 inches. Tibor De Nagy
Gallery, New York City.*)

Above:
ELEMENTAL
By William Muir (1902-   ), 1959.

A craftsman of high caliber, Muir has been closely associated with the Haystack Mountain School of Crafts on Deer Isle. (*Oak, 68 inches high. Collection of the artist.*)

MAINE LOBSTERMAN
By Charles Gordon Cutler (1914-   )

Local granite is a favorite medium of this sculptor, who has lived at South Brooksville for many years.
(*Granite, 17 inches high. Collection of the artist.*)

Right:
BOY
By Clark FitzGerald (1917-   ), 1955.

A versatile sculptor, Clark FitzGerald is best known for his figured architectural screens in churches, schools, and museums. (*Osage orangewood, 56 inches high. Collection of the artist.*)

Far right:
THE HARVESTER
By Abbott Pattison (1916-   ), 1962.

This plaster model, photographed on the artist's lawn, was made to be cast in bronze. (*Direct plaster figure, 82 inches high. Collection of the artist.*)

SUMMER IN THE TREES
By William Thon (1906-   ), 1958.
Here is a rich sensation of a pine wood; its shafts of light
and pockets of shadow, its jutting and receding branches
which the color quiets into a decorative surface.
*(Oil, 35¼ x 21¼ inches. The University Club, New York
City.)*

Opposite:
SPIRIT OF THE SEA
By William Zorach, 1962.
This figure is the artist's gift to the city of Bath, near which
he has lived for forty years. The reflecting pool and the
gardens which will eventually surround the fountain are
evidences of the thoroughness with which the Bath Gar-
den Club has carried through this project.
(Bronze, figure 84 inches high. City Park, Bath.)

FRESCOES, SOUTH SOLON
MEETING HOUSE
By students and faculty of the
Skowhegan School, 1952-1956.

The fresco on the end wall of this 1842
building is by William King, assisted by
Philip Bornath; it depicts the Flood and
scenes from the story of Moses. On the
side wall are frescoes of the Burning
Bush and the story of Job by Alfred
Blaustein. The ceiling by Edwin Brooks
has a symbol of the Godhead.

THE STORM WITHIN
By George Curtis (1921-   ), 1958.
This work, which the artist laid for the
photographer at the water's swirling edge,
is composed of the remains of a fish, a
lobster pot, and a net.
(Metal and wood, 7 inches high. Collection of the artist.)

Above:
CECILE PLAYING THE
RECORDER
By Milton E. Hebald (1917-   ), 1953.
In the background is the Bixler Art and
Music Center and the tower of the Miller
Library at Colby College.
*(Ceramic, 16½ inches high. Nordness
Gallery, New York City.)*

William Thon, a resident of Port Clyde, is among the best known of Maine artists whose styles are partially abstracted. Impressions of light, space, line, and mass are sensitively combined in his pictures of Maine woods. Laurence Sisson of Boothbay Harbor often tempers his more descriptive interests with similar infusions of the abstract.

As we look back over these artists who are unequivocally "modern"—Kienbusch, Heliker, Tam, Schoener, Muench, Thon, and others — we are as impressed by the effect on them of nature in general and Maine in particular as if we considered the men of a generation earlier — Marin or Hartley; of two generations — Bellows or Henri; of three — Homer; and on back in time through Lane and Birch to the beginning of our romantic era. One wonders if there is another region, excepting possibly certain spots on the French coast, which has had such a persistence of impact on generations of artists as has this Maine coast.

Our next step reminds us that no simple pattern can be expected in the evolution of art today. While the artists just considered have all developed from greater to less naturalism, there are others who are following the opposite path — away from abstraction. John Laurent, the son of Robert Laurent, also works in and near Ogunquit. Several years ago his paintings were strongly abstract, but today they are solidly representational. His "Steamed Clams," page 162, in the way it is composed reveals the freedom of the non-objective artist, but it is much concerned with the objects and their associations. Its rugged simplicity and rich paint are reminiscent of Hartley's work.

The distinctive thing about some of the representational art being done today is the way in which the broad color areas assert themselves as color and paint without losing their depictive function — or we might say, how they retain their force as color and paint while re-acquiring a depictive function. The work of Alex Katz, whose summers are spent near Lincolnville, is a good example of this. In it we feel a subtlety in the relations of sizes and colors of areas and in the way in which edges are treated. At first glance a picture like his of a Maine farmhouse, page 164, seems disarmingly simple, but on further acquaintance we sense its artfulness very much as we do with a painting by Manet. There are other young artists working in a way similar to Katz, and like him on a large scale, and of these we will probably hear more a few years hence.

Alex Katz's introduction to Maine was through the Skowhegan School of Painting and Sculpture, which has been responsible for bringing hundreds of art students and more than sixty visiting artists to the state. It was founded in 1946 with the distinct purpose of providing art students from all parts of the country the opportunity to study with American artists of stature. The permanent faculty for some years consisted of Henry Poor, his stepdaughter, Anne Poor, Charles Cutler, Sidney Simon, and Willard W. Cummings. The idea of such a school began with Willard Cummings, who had been brought up in Maine and saw the suitability of the rural setting near Lake Wesserunsett for it. He is himself a portraitist whose painting on page 160 of J. Seelye Bixler, now president-emeritus of Colby, is a decisive characterization of the sitter achieved through decisiveness in seeing forms and handling paint.

Of the many artists who visited Skowhegan as teachers, some left records of their coming that are part of the story of art in Maine. For example, Abraham Rattner did a powerfully expressive painting of the theme of farm machinery, and Edwin Dickinson painted his small but elegant "The Chair," which has all the finesse of handling for which he is well known.

Among sculptors we mention three who taught there more than one summer and who executed these examples in the lakeside setting of the school. Milton Hebald's "Cecile Playing the Recorder" is characteristic of his lively baroque-like figures which have gained him major commissions for architectural sculpture. Another artist associated with Skowhegan is Harold Tovish, whose sculpture has the sensitiveness of surface treatment which is one of the qualities of his art. And the well-known José de Creeft did some carving as well as teaching at the school.

One of the most ambitious undertakings of the Skowhegan School, and one which is notable because the advanced students themselves did the major part of the work, is the complete frescoing of the interior of the South Solon Meeting House, a church dating from the first half of the last century.

Evidence of the returning interest in the visible world may be seen among artists who have worked at Skowhegan. "The return to the figure" as it is sometimes called is in Maine more apt to be the "return to the scene." Characteristic are the flat areas of paint on a large canvas and an apparent casualness of execution obscuring a sensitive control of the relation between flat surface and represented depth. Artists working in this vein are John Guerin and Joseph Fiore.

Fairfield Porter is a veteran painter who has had long association with the Maine coast and whose work seems to gain stature each year. Sometimes simple static figures appear in the pictures which are placing Porter in the forefront of artists who merge the manipulative freedom characteristic of our time with a decisive selection of shapes and colors from reality. So, with Laurent, Katz, Dickinson, Guerin, Porter, and others, we find artists who are giving much attention to the visible world, though not in the same way as the detailed naturalists seen earlier. Ours is a rapidly evolving art and the patterns of evolution which are proceeding simultaneously sometimes move in opposite directions. This is not new in a world which is made up of different species evolving differently; the rapidity of the process, unfolding before our eyes, is what is new.

Among sculptors who are now at work in Maine there is a divergence of interest similar to that found among painters. Charles Gordon Cutler's "Maine Lobsterman" (page 166) belongs to the long tradition of the carving of granite which preserves its stony character and relates it to the ruggedness of the subject. George Curtis, in the sculpture shown on page 170, uses the newer technique of welded metal to record an equally native theme. There is a new approach to subject matter here — a reintroduction of the anecdote — and we look forward to the outcome of Curtis's approach in subsequent sculpture. Also a metal welder, but with opposite aims, is John Risley, who creates his intricate geometric constructions in the Belgrade Lakes region.

William Muir prefers wood for his freely shaped sculptures expressive of the organic world. The outward forms of trunks and limbs as well as their inner graining are the starting points for his art. With his painter-wife Muir lives at Stonington surrounded by nature, much of which makes its way into his work, but not as traditional representation.

Clark FitzGerald also lives at the sea's edge, at Castine, where he is kept busy executing commissions for churches and schools. The single figure, like the "Boy" on Page 167, is comparatively rare in his output. For his architectural work he prefers the flexibility and lightness of effect of the welded metal screen in which figures and symbols can be used with richness of form and of meaning.

The most forceful of the metal sculptors working today in Maine is Abbott Pattison, who has practiced his art in Lincolnville during the summers for many years. The human figure may often be partially hidden, but it plays a major role in his work. The other chief ingredients are the strong thrusts and counterthrusts which result from forms composed of bosses and hollows, prongs and apertures.

We close this section of our book with some feeling of inadequacy in attempting to give a just account of the art leading up to the present. There are facts which do not make themselves known and there is the difficulty of judging the art of today while keeping an outlook broad enough to include the diversity of styles and objectives. But one thesis, we feel sure, will stand the test of time as it has when applied to previous periods: that artists who have worked in Maine have felt the impress of a place and that their works, when gathered together, bear witness to this.

— JAMES M. CARPENTER

Public Museums
and Art Galleries
in Maine

It is appropriate to include in this book mention of the places where Maine art may be seen in the state itself.

In Portland the Museum of Art is open the year round and presents its permanent collection in its galleries and in the adjacent Sweat Mansion. Loan exhibitions and lectures supplement the museum's program. At Rockland the Farnsworth Library and Art Museum, under the direction of Mr. Wendell Hadlock, holds exhibitions throughout the year, and in the summer Maine artists are usually shown there.

The Walker Art Building in Brunswick houses the art museum of Bowdoin College. Professor Philip C. Beam is the director. Outstanding in the collection is the group of early American portraits, some of which are illustrated in this book. At Colby College in Waterville the art museum is located in the Bixler Art and Music Center. The American Heritage Collection of Folk Art is housed in Foss Hall. Professor James M. Carpenter is the director. The University of Maine at Orono has exhibitions of art in several buildings on campus, especially in Carnegie Hall. Professor Vincent Hartgen keeps up an active program of exhibiting contemporary art throughout the academic year and has supervised the acquisition of a remarkable collection of contemporary prints.

The Museum of Art of Ogunquit is open during the summer months. Both the permanent collection and special exhibitions each summer are devoted to American art of the twentieth century. The director, Mr. Henry Strater, is a painter himself, and

174

counts among his friends many of the twentieth-century artists included in this book. In Kennebunk the Old Brick Store Museum contains art and objects of local historical importance, and in the same block there is an art gallery and a display of Maine crafts. At Wiscasset the Lincoln County Cultural and Historical Association sponsors exhibitions of art of the past and present. The Old Jail contains historic objects, and in the newly renovated Custom House Gallery excellent exhibitions of contemporary painting and sculpture by Maine artists are held during the summer. Both of these, and other historical sites, have been developed under the superior guidance of Miss Mildred and Miss Madeline Burrage, whose contributions to art in Maine have been great.

The Penobscot Marine Museum in Searsport now occupies three buildings in which a permanent collection of all types of objects pertaining to the sea and ships is exhibited during the summer. Mr. Clifford Carver has been prominent among the many interested persons promoting this project.

In several localities the art associations exhibit the works of members during the summer months. One of the oldest of these is the Ogunquit Art Association, which holds exhibitions in the Barn Gallery. The Kennebec Valley Art Association has sponsored the Maine State Art Festival in the State House in Augusta for the past several summers.

In addition to the institutions mentioned above there are over sixty historical societies or groups devoted to the maintaining of historic houses. From the Lady Pepperrell House in Kittery to Burnham Tavern in Machias the persistent searcher will find examples of Maine art of varying quality. The Maine Historical Society, founded in 1822, maintains a collection of paintings and a large library at its quarters to the rear of the Longfellow House in Portland.

INDEX OF ARTISTS AND WORKS REPRODUCED

(Art works are identified by small capitals. Page numbers in italics refer to illustrations.)